Saving Seventeen

Saving Seventeen

Dr. Michael T. Mayo

Queens Army LLC   Tucson, Arizona

Copyright © 2020 by Michael T. Mayo

All rights are reserved. No part of this book may be copied, shared, stored, reproduced, or transmitted electronically or by any other means without explicit written permission from its creator Dr. Mayo.

ISBN 978-1-7345741-7-3

E-book ISBN 978-1-7345741-8-0

Library of Congress Control Number: 2020919607

Published by: Queens Army LLC

Our website is: queensarmy.net

Pictures on front and back covers are courtesy of PIXABAY

Distributed by Ingram

Date of first printing, November 2020

Contents

Dedication	9
Introduction	11
Dr. Mayo's Mantra	13
Teller of the Tale	14
When We Were Seventeen	15
Claire Davis	17
The Farmer in the Dell	19
Going Home	21
Baldwin & the Shebob	22
Ilana	25
Ivo & the Matchbox Rabbit	27
The Oracle & I: A Brief History	29
Flanders Fields	32
Tomb Stone	33
Candle Lights	34
Four Planes	37
Arvents	38
Bouncers	40
Distraction	40
A Window	42
Fire & Ice	45
Levantate Lazaro	49
Santori	50
Ghost at Grandma's House	52
Mina	54
Charmaine	55
Jo-Jo	59
Victoria	60
Ardyth Simpson	63
Thomas	65
Rankin	66
Emma	68
Flanagan's Folly	71
Alison	73
Selena	75

Deep Blue Sea	78
Chicago	80
Animal Shelter	82
Two Gold Coins	82
Blue Moon Two	84
Roberto Islas	86
Joseph Silverstein	87
Jonathan	89
Jeanie	93
Ram	95
Bus of No Return	98
Magic Mountain	100
The Spinnaker & the Imp	104
Beelzebub	107
Blue Goop	109
Untold Story	112
Irwin	116
The Taskmaster	120
Damian	123
The Night Bus, September 26th	125
The Oreo Brigade	127
Coyote's Howl	128
Tortuga	130
Smyth's	132
Maurice	137
The Return of the Three Crows	139
Where Wild Things Sleep	141
Emory	144
The Hounds of Baskerville	148
The Four Cardinal Wolves	150
Admissions & Omissions	152
Seeger & Seymour	154
The Night Bus	157
Speaking of Foxes	160
The Strings of Consternation	162
Izzy, Izzy...Izzy?	164
Worry-za-waste	165
Salis Burry	166

Boundary Layer Vortex	170
Zephyr	172
Beware... Beware	176
Canary Road	180
Rainy Day	184
Door to Tomorrow	186
At the End of the Rainbow	188
Hope is Not a Strategy!	191
The Last Row	193
12:59...Roger...Rabbit	196
An open letter to anyone who has a Mother	198
Making Smoke	200
Red Face, Red Man	202
Wararies	203
The Spirit in the Pot	207
Indian in a Pot	209
Long Bow	212
Heart of Gold	214
Itsacono	217
The State of Affairs	220
De – Termination	222
Adept's School of Knowledge	225
Hidden Arena	227
Into the Light	230
Illusion	232
Sleeping Buddha	236
Seven Minds	239
Death's Door	245
Tytus	248
The Golden Fly	250
The Ram's Horn	252
Car Seventeen	254
Talkin'... Robin...	257
Night Train to Heaven	259
Robin's Return	261
Cousins	263
Rescue Mission	265
Abu Dhabi	272

Ashes…Ashes…We All Fall down!	274
Battleship Blue	276
The Hitch Hiker	279
The Last Stop	282
Spindle & Glide	284
Key Stone	285
Sands of Time	287
Sepulcher	289
Destiny	290
Stairway to Heaven	291
Holy Water	293
Sharon	294
Itsacano Again	296
Quadrivium	297
Books by: Dr. Mayo	301
About Dr. Mayo	303
Seventeen Incarnations	304

Dedication

This book is dedicated to all of our families and friends, who have made us who we really are.

Introduction

After I rescued someone several years ago, the Source said that I needed to "Save seventeen".

This became the name for this book. The Source didn't specify which or what seventeen I should save but just to "Save seventeen". I didn't discover which "seventeen" or what "seventeen" I needed to save until the book was complete.

These recounts are of efforts I made to save seventeen others and myself in the process.

Dr. Mayo's Mantra

Nothing is what it appears to be, ever.

Don't take it personally, even if it's meant to be.

Every challenge brings an opportunity. (a gift).

The secret is to focus on the opportunity...
　　Not on the challenge.

Expect nothing,
　　and you will never be disappointed.

The only thing between you, and your dreams,
　　is you.

Give yourself permission to fail... So you can
　　give yourself permission to succeed.

Treat yourself the way you want others
　　to treat you.

Learn to say 'Thank You,' and mean it.

Forgive others...
　　So you can forgive yourself.

Teller of the Tale

At the heart of every story is the teller of the tale.

When We Were Seventeen

My son called on Monday with a special request. He told me that a lady there had a stroke and was currently on life support in the hospital. They were going to discontinue life support for her that evening. He wanted me to offer her assistance with her crossing over. I told him that I would do what I could.

My normal protocol is first to summon that individual to where I am, to begin the transition. When I did so, a very frail decrepit old lady hobbled toward me. She was unresponsive and appeared to be only partially there. After an extensive period, I abandoned that effort which had been to no avail. The second step involves me going to where that person is currently located. I waited a few hours for any aberrations I might have created to dissipate then I went to where she currently was.

I found her sitting on the side of the road. She was very disoriented and very upset. She was also very young. She told me that she was seventeen and she looked it. Her name was Margaret. She was lost and wanted to go home but she couldn't provide any useful information that could help me take her to where she needed to be. After much effort, I finally gave up and decided to take her to Never Land to give her a chance to rest and recover.

A couple of days later, I went to Never Land to see how she was doing. She wasn't any better. The next night I returned and escorted her to where Baldwin had created his magical fire pit, lit the fire, wrapped Margaret up in a borrowed blanket and left her watching the flickering flames, in the hope that this would help her to settle down but when I returned several hours later she was staring into the fire like a 'Podling' staring at the 'Dark Crystal'. I knew then this would require me to use a different strategy.

Margaret, the old lady, wasn't all there and Margaret, the seventeen-year old young girl, wasn't all there either. I reasoned that perhaps she was partially in two separate places and I would need to get the two parts of her back together before we would be able to make any real progress.

I summoned Margaret, the old lady, and escorted her into Never Land, put them together in front of the fire but again that was to no avail. Then I understood that her personality and her life had been split apart when she was seventeen. I took the two of them over the bridge and out of Never Land. I located the 'Door of No Return' and we went through that doorway. Inside, their two previously separated personalities were irreversibly reunited back into one.

Together we emerged, Margaret and I. Again I asked her where she wanted to go. Margaret continued to insist that she wanted to go to when she was seventeen. Finally I understood that the place she wanted to be was where and when she was seventeen. I took her hand and we crossed over into that place, the place she was when she was seventeen.

Margaret smiled then turned towards me, gave me

a big hug and said, "Thank you so much for taking us back to when we were seventeen". Somehow, I too was also, just seventeen.

Claire Davis

What a magnificent specimen! It is indeed an amazing tale that entangled the two of us. I am willing to tell the tale, if you have the patience to persevere in its telling.

I heard on the news there had been yet another school shooting. This one was at Arapajo High School in Colorado. It resulted in the suicide of the shooter and critical injury to another student. A third student had minor injuries.

These events are quite unsettling to every parent. Each of us would want to do whatever we could to ameliorate these situations. So, I did what I thought was appropriate, I did what I was capable of doing. I summoned the consciousness of Claire Davis. She was the seventeen year-old student who was in the hospital in critical condition from a shotgun blast to the head at close range.

I summoned her from wherever she was and took her to Never Land. She was confused and completely disoriented. Spending a few days in a protected environment like Never Land would give her a chance to rest and recuperate.

Two days later I went back to Never Land and took

Claire for a short walk to see how well she was doing. She had made friends with some of the local residents there and was in a much improved mental state but she was not yet ready for the cold, hard facts regarding the reality of her situation.

The next evening I returned to Never Land. Claire and I made our way to where Baldwin the dwarf had camped out during his brief stay in Never Land. He had made a magical fire pit that could be rekindled with a focused mind. We sat in the darkness. I rekindled the flames in the fire pit and then I began to share some of the realities of her situation with her. I told her that she had been injured and was currently in the critical-care ward of the hospital. I wasn't sure about the specifics of her injuries but her prognosis was not great. She needed to be aware of the situation and to start considering her options because at some point she would have to decide exactly what she wanted to do. We sat there in silence watching the dancing flames for some time before I escorted her back to where she was staying with a family there in Never Land. Then, I left.

The next night I returned to Never Land to check on Claire. I borrowed a blanket and took it with us back to the magical fire pit where I rekindled the fire and wrapped her up in the blanket as we sat with our backs against the trunk of a large fallen tree. I gave her more complete details about the gravity of her condition because I had visited her in the hospital and the situation was not good. I told her that the life she had known was over. If she survived, she would be dependent, debilitated, and deformed. She would not be intellectually intact and probably unable to see, or communicate with those she loved. Her other options were to die, to live in Never Land or to become a citizen in the new Glen which was currently being reconstructed. It would be a place of mystery and magic where she would become a princess.

I left her there in front of the flames alone, to contemplate her pending decisions.

The Farmer in the Dell

It was completely dark as I crossed back over the bridge from Never Land. As soon as I stepped off of the bridge, a short plump man with a pitchfork appeared from nowhere, right in front of me, directly in my path. He wore denim overalls, a plaid flannel shirt. He had a wide-brimmed straw hat on his head. His skin was snow white. His cheeks and nose were rosy, like Santa Claus but without spectacles or a beard. I asked him who he was.

"I'm The Farmer in the Dell," he said most emphatically. "Really?" I said, "Where did you come from?" He told me that he came from Fantasy Land and asked if I would like to see his farm in the Dell. I told him, "Sure, let's go." So we went to his farmhouse in the Dell. I met his wife Shirley. He introduced himself as Bill, and I got the grand tour from them.

I went down to their basement. He called it their root

cellar. There I saw potatoes, cabbage, turnips, onions, squash, beans, corn, and wheat. Shirley showed me jars of pickles, tomatoes, fruits, jams, jellies, smoked sausages, bacon and hams. They had flour, cornmeal, molasses, and honey, cheeses and dried fruits. Shirley even gave me some fresh baked bread with preserves to try. They were delicious.

They showed me the barn and the barnyard with all of the animals: the pigs, the black and white Holstein cows, the Red Leghorn chickens, their plow horses, the sheep and goats and even their big, fluffy brown family dog. I asked if they had any ducks or geese. They said only the wild ones down on their small lake. They had some turkeys but just a few and only one tom. I thanked them for their hospitality and promised I would stop by again sometime soon for a friendly visit.

The next morning I went back to the farm in the Dell to visit with the farmer Bill and his wife Shirley. They weren't there. The front door was unlocked. I went looking for them throughout their house. I even went to the basement. There was nothing there. All of the things, which had been there, were gone. The cupboard was literally bare. I went to the barn. It was completely empty. All of the animals from the barnyard were missing. Even their big, brown fluffy dog had vanished. Only the wild ducks and geese remained on their small lake. From there, I went to the bridge to Never Land and crossed over looking for Clare. She had also vanished, leaving behind only a crumpled blanket on the ground by the fallen tree trunk, next to the fire pit, which was still smoldering.

Then it became clear to me that Clare Davis had chosen to return to be with her adoptive parents in Colorado despite the prospect that she would probably not survive and she would have a terrible life of difficulty, debility and dependence if she actually did survive. She was their "Farmer's Daughter." They were for Clare, "The Farmer in the Dell and his wife Shirley." They were Clare's fantasy family. They were Clare's own creation from her childhood memories.

Going Home

We returned home from California on the 28th of December. I read in one of the old newspapers the next morning that Claire Davis, the 17 year-old Colorado high school senior, shooting victim, had passed away from her injuries. I went looking for her the evening of the 29th. I found her sitting outside of the hospital, on the curb, with her head hung low, supported by both hands. She was very despondent. I took her hand and we started walking. I reminded her that it was time to choose where she wanted to go. She could go with her death or she could go to Never Land or she could have a new beginning in a place of mystery and magic where she would be a princess.

She straightened her posture, smiled coyly and looked me straight in the eye, shaking her head slowly up and down in the affirmative. I opened the portal that would take her to her new home and a new beginning. I whispered the name of the one she should ask for into her left ear. Claire turned and stepped into the portal and vanished.

I did what any parent would have tried to do. I gave Claire the chance to grow up and to be a princess.

I checked in with the Wizard of the Glen. He told me that Claire had taken the new name of Pricilla Michaels, in honor of both her adoptive father, whom she dearly loved and admired and me, for arranging her a new beginning and a new life as Princess Pricilla of the Glen and for her beautiful new castle.

Baldwin & the Shebob

This morning at 3:00 a.m., my wife woke me up saying there was something there in the bedroom. I told her O.K., I would check it out. These things always seem to appear only on her side of the bed.

Standing inside of the doorway to our bedroom was this huge 'Grim Reaper'. He was at least seven feet tall, dressed in a hooded black robe that pooled on the floor covering his feet. In his right hand, he held up a scythe with a jagged blade that was at least four feet in length. The wooden handle made the scythe even taller than he was. He stood motionless looking straight at me. I thought, "This does not look good."

I asked him what he was doing there in my bedroom. He didn't answer. I asked if he could speak. He removed his hood, revealing a perfectly formed complete skull, perfect and completely black. He said nothing. Then, he re-covered his head with his hood.

On the corner of the bed were two strange looking hands, with short stubby fingers and squashed fingertips with darkened wooden fingernails. The creature had a really weird, round, wooden, head. When I asked what it wanted, its hands began shuffling down the edge of the bed towards my wife, as though they were walking, while the head itself bobbed from side to side. I said clearly to this creature, "Please come to my side of the bed." It abruptly stopped, then moved around to my side of the bed. I was looking directly at its perfectly round head. All of its features appeared to be painted on. It had two round red balls painted on its cheeks, two unblinking, round black eyes, two ears painted flat against the sides of its round skull, and a strange little truncated hat upon its head. There was no neck. The round head sat squarely upon a perfectly round body with painted German-style short pants with wide straps going over each shoulder and a short sleeve white shirt decorated with buttons going down the front and a starched collar, all painted on. Its arms and legs seemed very stiff and barely functional.

After making several attempts to communicate with this strange creature, I decided to try something novel. I recently acquired a supply of Fairy Dust. It was actually obtained on Monday and this was Saturday. I knew Fairy Dust had magical powers but not exactly what those powers were. I sprinkled some dust over this thing. It immediately morphed into a very old, rugged-looking dwarf, complete with long scraggly beard, crumpled pointed hat with its wide brim and floppy top and a tattered, dirty-brown robe that covered his feet. I asked if he was a dwarf. He nodded yes. I asked if he were dead or alive. He retorted, "Well, what do you think?" I said that I didn't know for sure because I can't always be certain if a magical creature is really dead or actually alive.

I asked if someone had perhaps cast a spell upon him. He said that a powerful enchantress had bewitched him and turned him into a Shebob. I looked down on the floor beside him where a painted wooden toy figure now lay. I asked if that toy were a Shebob. He said that it was. He told me that his name was Baldwin, that he was over 500 years old and that the Grimm Reaper was a friend of his. The Grimm Reaper told Baldwin that he had heard of a powerful sorcerer who could break the enchantment and that he would find that sorcerer and take him there. Apparently, I am that sorcerer.

I asked Baldwin where he needed to go. He told me that he was exhausted and needed some rest. I escorted Baldwin over the bridge into Never Land, introduced him to Jenkins, one of the leprechauns, asked him to show Baldwin around and introduce him to all of the magical creatures there in Never Land. I told Baldwin that I would return after he was rested and arrange for safe passage for him to any place or time that he desired.

I returned to our bedroom. The 'Grimm Reaper' was

still standing in the doorway. I told him that Baldwin was safe in Never Land and I would see to his safe return when he was again ready to travel. The Grimm Reaper nodded his head in approval, turned and disappeared swiftly down our hallway.

Ilana

I was engaged in working within the event horizon, surveying the open area where the fog had been lifted and the surface of the sea was smoothed. This limited perspective of future events allows an observer to focus more clearly on a single event, without the confusion that accompanies multiple events unfolding simultaneously. The edge of the water was a few feet behind me. A short distance away, in the water, floating towards my foot was what appeared to be that funny little hat which the Shebob had worn on its head. As the hat drifted closer to my foot, I noticed a round dark something moving towards me from deep water. My first instinct was to get out of the water as fast as I could. But, being curious, I instead put on those rose-colored glasses, which allow me to see things as they really are, instead of what they might otherwise appear to be.

The hat immediately became a small fairy with a tiny magic wand and the dark object approaching from beneath the water, became some sort of black torpedo-like thing heading straight towards me at increasing speed. I placed the small fairy on my left shoulder. She grew into a full size Fairy, pointed her wand at the approaching object and blasted it to pieces. I said to her "Wow...That was so great. What was that thing?"

The fairy told me that it was the wicked enchantress, who had turned Baldwin into a Shebob, and that the enchantress was coming to get me for having broken her spell that she had placed on the dwarf, Baldwin. I thanked the fairy for her help and asked her what her name was? She told me that she was the fairy Ilana. Then she vanished without a trace.

From there I went to check on Baldwin in Never Land. It had been four days since I escorted him there and left him to recover from his travails as the enchanted Shebob. I crossed the bridge into Never Land and began the search to find him. I finally found him deep in the forest sitting in front of a magical fire, smoking his pipe. It was early in the morning and still completely dark outside. I asked Baldwin why he wasn't asleep. He said that he hadn't slept at all in the last four days because he was afraid that the wicked enchantress would find him and turn him back into the Shebob.

When I told him what had just happened, he was elated. "You know Ilana," he asked? "I do now," I said. Baldwin said that he hated that hat and never touched it. He was amazed that the secret to his escape sat squarely on his own head the whole time but he failed to recognize it and he failed to have hope. "You need to rest up, and then decide to where and to when you need to go and I will get you there, somehow. I'll be back in a few days to check on you," I said. Then I returned to my own time and place in normal reality, perchance to have 'just another normal day'.

Ivo & the Matchbox Rabbit

I wanted to visit Baldwin the dwarf. Instead of opening a portal that can create a disturbance in the time space continuum, I went by the Night Bus. It arrived right on time at two o'clock in the morning. I greeted Brad Raccoon, the driver of the Night Bus, as I climbed into the bus and told him where I wanted to go. In the wink of an eye we arrived at Baldwin's front gate. It took a few minutes for Baldwin to answer my clanging on his iron knocker but his front door finally began to open and Baldwin greeted me with a big smile as he squinted at me through his sleepy eyes.

We politely exchanged greetings before getting down to the business at hand. After much deliberation, I finally convinced Baldwin to accompany me on an adventure to seek my fortune. Baldwin gathered a few essentials, like his pipe, his reading glasses, his walking stick and a pouch of embers from the hearth of his fireplace with which to kindle a fire. Our first stop would be in Ireland to visit the wizard.

When we stepped out of the portal in Ireland, where the wizard was finishing his renovation of the Glen, it was still dark. The sun had yet to come up. We had arrived unexpectedly and with such little disturbance that the wizard was still asleep in his tree. As I approached his tree, two eyes popped open, staring out at me through the rough bark. He separated himself from the tree itself and emerged, leaving a large crack in the side of the tree where he had moments before been sleeping.

The wizard asked why we were there. When I told him that we had come seeking our fortune, he squinted his eyes until they were almost closed and hummed to himself for a moment before asking "What fortune might that be?" We both told him we had no idea. That was why we were here seeking his advice. He suggested that we sit down next to the tall fir tree and meditate upon the issue until we came up with an answer. Baldwin fell asleep quickly. I meditated until the sun began to rise, then I got anxious and decided to check out the progress that Merlin had made thus far in renovating the Glen. The place was picture perfect. As I made my way down the bank, towards the tinkling stream, I spied a matchbox. Matches seemed somehow so out of place here. I picked up the matchbox, opened it expecting to find a trove of wooden matches inside but there to my surprise sat the smallest rabbit you could ever imagine. I asked the rabbit what it was doing in a matchbox. The rabbit told me that it lived there in the matchbox. That was his home. When I asked where he had come from, he told me that he belonged to Ivo the Giant. "Are there giants in the Glen?" I asked.

"No," the rabbit said. "Ivo was curious about the Glen. He must have accidently dropped the matchbox while he was exploring." "You are so small," I said. "Perhaps, you might be happier with leprechauns."

"Leprechauns?" He retorted. "Do you know where there are leprechauns?"

I told the Matchbox Rabbit that a whole family composed of three generations of leprechauns lived near me in my home far across the sea.

"I use to live with leprechauns before they all disappeared from the Glen and Ivo the Giant took me away to 'Giant Land'. Do you think I could go and live with the family of leprechauns who live near you?"

"Of course," I said. And then, I took the rabbit across the sea and introduced him to Jenkins and his entire family of leprechauns. That was where the matchbox rabbit chose to stay. I returned to Ireland. Baldwin was still sleeping against that same tree.

The Oracle & I: A Brief History

We first met about twenty years ago when I began to time travel. He lived some 2700 years ago. The Oracle lived in a cave complex on the side of a cliff overlooking the Adriatic Sea. He was not blind at birth but became blind while still a young boy. Because he was blind, he was left in the midst of women, girls and young children, while the other boys were introduced to the world of men. One young girl was given primary responsibility for his care. Over time, they became constant companions and intimate friends.

When she became of age, her father sold her to a traveling merchant where she became the youngest of his growing harem. The emotional trauma from this loss of his constant companion and only confidant drove him to seek refuge in the solitude of the caves where he became a hermit. There he survived on the donations of food from those seeking council. By the time I encountered him, he had acquired the wisdom and knowledge for which he garnered the title of 'The Oracle'.

After many years of wandering the realms of other realities, I acquired many magic potions, charms and spells. On one visit with the Oracle, I tried out a new one on the Oracle and it restored his sight. Immediately, upon the return of his vision, the Oracle left in search of the girl lost from his childhood.

Black Beard brought the Oracle and me back to the caves of the Oracle's past. Here was where I was supposed to begin the quest for my fortune. The Oracle wanted me to begin mastering the art of the oracle by assuming his role as Oracle while he observed from the darkness of his cave.

The first who came seeking council was an elderly man with the trappings of great wealth. He brought a large platter of food as a gift for the Oracle. He assumed that I was the 'Blind Oracle of the Caves'. The only light in the cave came from a single candle sitting on a rock outcropping between us. I asked why he had come. The Merchant said that he was seeking peace of mind because his sleep of late had been much disturbed.

I asked the merchant, "Why have you come with deceit in your heart. Deceit is something one might expect from a spurned woman but never from a man of honor. You have brought delicacies laced with poison in hopes of causing me great personal harm. What have I done to thusly be rewarded? You think that because you are sighted that you have great advantage. You think me blind and disadvantaged. You come with dagger hidden beneath your vest. You think me to be a blind beggar but truth and honor are more powerful than deceit and dagger. Enter the blind man's world of darkness."

With a puff of air, I extinguished the candle's flame and with a whack from my trusty walking stick, I rendered the traveling merchant unconscious. I dragged him to the cave's entrance and heaved him over the edge onto the rocky shore far below. I took his platter of poisoned delicacies and tossed them to him lying there far below.

I turned to the Oracle and said, "I have not killed him. He was quite alive when he left my company. Perhaps he stumbled over that first step or perhaps he fell upon his own dagger or perhaps he consumed some tainted morsels of food or perhaps he died from the self-inflicted wounds of deceit and dishonor, for those will surely kill any man."

The great irony was that this wealthy man was the traveling merchant who purchased the Oracle's childhood girl friend and caregiver those many years ago. The merchant had come intent on killing the Oracle but had the misfortune of encountering a time traveling sorcerer from far in the future.

Flanders Fields

I was walking with the Source last night. He asked me if I knew where we were. I told the Source that I had no idea where we were. He said, "In Flanders Fields". As we walked along wisps of smoke puffed out of the ground and shot up into the night sky. He asked me if I knew what all those wisps of smoke were. Again I told him that I had no idea. The Source said they were the spirits of soldiers who died in World War I. He said that he had been here many times before encouraging these many departed young soldiers to come out from hiding in their respective shallow graves but none would ever do so because they felt guilty and were too afraid of what the Source might do to them to leave the safety of their respective graves but when I accompanied the Source, they quickly came forth and departed for their unknown futures because they felt safe in my presence. I have no idea why that would be the case. After the Source departed, leaving me alone in Flanders Fields, I continued to walk the entire area where all of these spirits have remained for the past hundred years. With my passing they continued to pour forth from beneath the green grasses, where poppies once grew, there in 'Flanders Fields'.

I chanced upon the grave of one, Tyler Moore,

dead by age seventeen. That seemed very young to me to come to the end of one's life so violently and so young. I was drawn to this particular grave by a sense of great sadness and futility. As I contemplated Tyler's passing at such a young age I sensed movement out of the corner of one eye. I asked perchance could that be the ghost of Tyler Moore. The answer came back as a "Yes". He lied to get into the army and died not as the hero he envisioned but as a gut-shot kid sorrowful and fearful of death's coming. He never forgave himself for the untold sadness his pointless demise inflicted upon his mother and his friends. I assured him that they were all now, long since dead and buried and surely awaiting his arrival where they would rejoice at his homecoming. Excited he departed, last of all in leaving 'Flanders Fields', where poppies once grew.

Tomb Stone

I was shocked when I saw concession number ninety. Innocence and I were holding hands but I was still shocked by what I saw. The whole concession was a huge rectangular hole in the ground with a giant white marble tombstone sticking up in back of it. The top was round. The message was clear, R.I.P. There was no name on it. I assumed it would be my grave. We always assume the worst. That seems to be Human nature, "Always think the worst". I asked Innocence what he saw. He said he saw a wide muddy river with families standing on the other side, old men, children, women holding tiny babies. I asked the Source for some kind of explanation. He told me what the point of the grave at concession ninety was.

He said, "Today is the seventy-fifth anniversary of the battle for 'Iwo Jima'. More than seven thousand American soldiers perished here and close to twenty thousand Japanese soldiers died here as well. It was brutal hand-to-hand combat."

I was there. I could see Mount Suribachi in the distance as plain as day. The Source said my task now was to liberate all the remaining souls still stranded here after seventy-five years. As we traversed back and forth over the caves and battlegrounds, the lost souls poured fourth beginning their long-delayed journeys to rejoin their respective families.

This reminded me of the magic in 'Flanders Fields'.

Candle Lights

Innocence and I visited concession ninety-one, last night. The entire concession was jammed pack full of people all holding up an unlit candle in a glass jar high above their bowed heads. Nothing was in color. Everything was in shades of gray. These were like the ones you light at church and place in front of a religious statue. This made no sense to me.

We hung around there for a while but nothing was happening so we left and were going to go back later. I had another project that I was working on. I was looking for an individual by the name of Kurt Nacionales. He was a mentally disturbed young man who had apparently attempted to commit suicide in his parent's home but had not been successful. I became involved with this project when the young couple that rented that house were having problems with spirits or ghosts. They asked me to get rid of whatever was causing problems for them in that rental property.

When I went there a few days ago it was a little after one o'clock in the morning. This fairly large young man came down the hall towards me. He didn't look or behave like a ghost. He appeared to be in his late twenty's or early thirty's. His hair was dirty blond with a tinge of red, a little on the long side and wavy but not quite curly. I thought he might be Kurt. I tried to get his attention and called him by name but he rushed right by me and went into the bathroom and was rummaging around.

I came to get rid of whatever was there so I stuffed him into this leather bag I carry that puts things into suspended animation. When I started dragging him outside I discovered he was quite heavy. That meant he wasn't a ghost or a spirit. He had to be something that had physical properties and could obviously interact with physical things like a poltergeist or a 'Freddy Kruger' or some other strange thing I wasn't familiar with. I didn't know what to do with it so I took it home and dumped it in my front yard under an apple tree. I made several inquiries in an attempt to learn more about what I was dealing with but to no avail. I was advised to, "let sleeping dogs lie."

When I finally encountered Kurt Nacionales, I knew immediately what had happened. Somehow before, during or after the suicide attempt, Kurt's body had been taken over by a demon of some kind. I think it was a Wraith. Its glowing yellow eyes and shadowy presence engulfed what remained of Kurt's physical body. What I previously encountered in the hall and now held in a leather bag on ice was the fragmented body and soul of Kurt. So what I did was to force the 'Cross of Palmero' onto his forehead. He writhed in pain and fell backwards. I then forced the mystic 'Celtic Cross' onto his forehead and as he stumbled backwards, I hurtled a psychic explosive device at him. When it exploded, Kurt fell limp to the floor and the demon departed.

I took Kurt's limp body and stuffed it into the leather bag where the rest of his fragmented soul was, then pushed the bag with both parts of him through the 'Door of No Returns' where the separate parts would be reunited. From there I took the bag with Kurt still inside and returned to concession ninety-one. As I descended down onto the concession I dumped the bag. All of the candles in all of the glass jars lit up at once. All of their prayers for Kurt had been answered. He flew off into the physical world and is now alive and well, no longer insane, and no longer possessed by the demonic Wraith.

I asked Innocence what he had seen. He told me that

when we first arrived, the throng of people all held up white crosses high in the air with their heads bowed in prayer. When their prayers were answered each cross became a yellow flower and all of the flowers flew up into the air and coalesced into a handsome young man, a man named Kurt Nationales.

There must have been magic in all those lighted candles, fervent prayers and yellow flowers.

Four Planes

A week ago, the Source asked me to go with him.

We were moving along through the space between the clouds above and the towns and landscape below. I estimated we were about three or four thousand feet above ground level. He called this space the 'Astral Plane'. From there we moved up into the clouds. The Source called this area where clouds are located, the 'Celestial Plane'. As we moved even higher he referred to the area above where clouds form as, the 'Heavenly plane'. The last area above the atmosphere he referred to as the 'Inter stellar plane'.

Years ago, I spent a great deal of time learning to navigate the Astral Planes and became quite proficient with astral projection. When I mentioned this to the Source he said this, "There are several layers in the Astral Plane. Each layer is different and each layer is unique. You may have noticed that we were moving very rapidly through that space but there was no effect from the wind." I did notice that and I did think that was odd because in the past when I was doing a lot of astral projection, the wind was always a limiting factor and speeds above ninety miles per hour were difficult to maintain unless you went even higher up into the atmosphere. He said that the Astral Plane was where worldly affairs unfolded. The Celestial plane was the domain of angels while the Heavenly Plane was the domain of the Gods & Demi-Gods. He did point out that Heaven itself was separate and not located in the Heavenly Plane. At the time this little excursion made no sense to me. I didn't get the point of it.

Arvents

Last night when I went to the 'Place' to recharge my energy supply the Source said that he wanted to show me something. He asked me to look down and tell him what I saw. We were a couple thousand feet up above looking down on the roofs and yards of a suburban neighborhood. He left it at that. A couple of hours later, the 'Source took me back to the very same spot high in the air above those same houses and told me there was something in one of the houses that he pointed out to me and he wanted me to go down and get whatever was in there, out of the house. So I did.

When I went in through the garage. I could see ten bony fingers sticking out over the edge of a piece of furniture located there. I figured I would come back later and deal with whatever that happened to be but I needed to check out the whole house first to determine what was actually there before I took any definitive action. I encountered something in the dining area next to the kitchen that looked like a giant tennis ball the size of a beach ball with two skinny bird legs and two spaghetti arms with ten bony fingers, five on each of its two bony hands.

I gave warning that I was going to detonate a large explosive device that would blast it and any other things completely out of the house if whatever was there didn't come forward immediately. These things began to emerge from different areas of the house. There were seven of them in all. There were two 'Adults', two 'Women' and three 'children', whatever that meant. They identified themselves as 'Arvents'. They were khaki-colored and had two eyes, a tiny nose and a good size mouth. They reminded me of 'Mike' from the movie "Monsters Incorporated".

I didn't have any idea what they were capable of doing but they all seemed to be congenial enough so I took them over to my son's house in Orange County and told them not to bother anyone. I said they could stay in the basement or in the upstairs area above the garage as long as they didn't cause any trouble. I needed some time to figure out what I was going to do with them and check with the 'Source' about their current situation.

Bouncers

Last night when I was talking with the 'Source' he said we needed to take the 'Bouncers' to a safe place for them to stay. Apparently the Source referred to these Arvents as 'Bouncers'. We went over and picked up the Arvents. He referred to them again as Bouncers. They looked like giant tennis balls so calling them bouncers seemed to be O.K. to me. We took off with them to somewhere. We approached an island that looked very familiar. When we got closer I recognized it as 'Goat Island'. I have been there many times before. The 'Source' said the Father needed to stay on the beach but the rest of the Bouncers should stay in a cave. After he left us there, I asked the Arvents why the 'Source' called them bouncers.

They told me that the 'Source' would take them where there had been a loss of life, a tragedy or a great disaster and they would help the survivors to 'Bounce Back' and resume living. I found it hard to believe I had played a role in this seemingly 'grand scheme'.

Distraction

Last night the Source took me to a location a few hundred feet above the ground. It was at night and the area was near a park. There was a sidewalk with grass between the road and the walkway next to the park.

Street lamps were scattered here and there but the area was not well lit. A man wearing a beige trench coat and fedora hat was walking alone along the sidewalk. He was wearing dark sunglasses and his hands were stuffed into the pockets of his coat. The Source said to me, "Distract him."

So, I dropped down onto the sidewalk twenty or thirty feet in front of the stranger, as a Grizzly Bear. The man immediately stopped, pulled out a revolver and fired a round at me. Before the bullet reached me, I shape-shifted into a large Anaconda several feet to my left and the bullet missed completely. He fired again and I shape-shifted into a Bengal Tiger, again another miss. I shape-shifted into a huge gorilla. Another shot and another miss. I shape-shifted into two gorillas, more shots more misses. Next I shape-shifted into a sorcerer with glowing red eyes wearing a drab gray wool robe, holding a magic staff and a floppy pointed hat, more shots. The hat and robe fell empty in a pile to the ground. I shape-shifted into Constantine, my sword held high. The stranger turned and fled, looking back over his shoulder. Distracted, he ran in front of an oncoming speeding car. He was killed instantly. Out of his body flew a devil, escaping into the night. The body of a possessed man lay lifeless in the street still grimly illuminated in the car light.

The Source was very pleased. He said, "That was your test. You did well."

A Window

At 3:07 this morning I was awake wondering if I would ever be able to get back to sleep again. I engaged the Facilitator, who said that he wanted to show me a window. It sounded O.K. to me. He took me a short distance away to the wooden frame around a window but there was no glass in it. The frame was made of heavy oak stained and varnished. It was about 4 feet high and 5 or 6 feet wide. I stood in front of the window frame looking out onto a scene with a dark background. A long, single line of people were slowly winding their way from the right side to the left side.

The line was made up of men and women following each other closely, as they progressed across the space framed by the window. They all wore dark clothing and they all had a hat or scarf or some sort of covering on their heads. At the very end of the line on the left side stood a single figure accepting each passerby's head covering before they jumped and disappeared into an abyss. As each jumper surrendered their headwear, the gender and face of the person accepting these coverings changed. The collector tossed the head dress into the abyss, smiled and then, the jumper jumped.

On the right side where the line was forming, new entrants came forward from every direction, falling into the procession as it continued to form. I proceeded back towards the beginnings of the line and found a female sojourner that had clothing that looked rather sturdy, reasonably nice looking and not too old or too decrepit.

I latched onto her jacket with a strong grip and followed her to the jumping off point. When we arrived at the front of the line, the face of the character receiving head cover changed to that of an older lady who appeared as though she might have been this jumper's mother. She smiled at us and we jumped into the abyss.

We floated down through clouds into a scene from maybe the 1930's or 40's, landing softly. I walked a few paces behind the lady dressed in her dark business skirt and jacket. She was still wearing the small black hat with mesh on one side, which partially covered her face. A passerby said, "Good morning Mrs. Eber". Mrs. Eber returned the good morning and proceeded to the front door of a clothing establishment where she produced the key and made her way into the store. I followed closely behind her. She didn't seem to even notice my presence. She went to the back of the store, placed her hat on its mannequin, then sat down at her desk and began methodically going through a stack of papers, subsequently placing each in turn into a bin on the right side of her desk.

After going through several papers she hesitated, staring at this 'one' in particular for an extended period of time. Mrs. Eber slowly lowered the paper to the desktop, opened the desk drawer, pulled out a revolver, put it to her temple, and pulled the trigger. Instead of a loud bang, we were instantly transported to the back of that same line, as it reformed.

The process started over again with every element of the experience being repeated exactly, only this time

I noticed which particular piece of paper resulted in Mrs. Eber shooting herself.

We went back to the end of the line, back to the beginning of the line, back to the "Good morning Mrs. Eber" but when she began going through the papers this time, I snatched that one page away and crumpled it up in my hand. Mrs. Eber finished going through her pile of papers, removed her jacket and then proceeded to the counter in the front of her store where she began greeting would-be customers politely when they entered. Mrs. Eber was back in business.

I opened the drawer in the desk slowly, removed the revolver and placed it in my pocket. I went to the window where there was more light, un-crumpled the paper and read it:

Dear Marion,
It is with great sadness that I must inform you that your son Charles has passed this day.
He was improving daily. We had great hopes for his early and complete recovery and looked forward to his rapid return, once again to your family...

With sincerest sympathy,
Dr. Franklin

This continuing repetition, which had been going on for perhaps 75 years, of Mrs. Eber's 'Ground Hog's Day' was interrupted by those actions which I had taken.

She could always receive another letter or phone

call. She could always get another revolver. But, she didn't get that letter and she didn't use that gun, because of the action, which I took.

After this experience was complete, I asked the Facilitator, what was the point of all of that. He said, "The window was a window of opportunity to intervene on behalf of another, to make a difference, and to save someone from a needless suicide."

Fire & Ice

10/27/15

This morning I was awake at 1:47 a.m. I asked the Source if there were anything he thought I should look into. He said I should go to the 'Place of Tanning'. He said, "Tell that raccoon bus driver, on the Night Bus, to take you to the 'Place of Tanning.' You are ready to go there." Then he told me that it wasn't what I thought it would be but that he was curious as to what I would make of it.

So, before the Night Bus arrived at 2:00 a.m. I thought that I should take a few things with me. I went to the garage and got my windbreaker, which is a bright yellow. I checked to see if the cotton gloves were still in one of the pockets. On my way past the refrigerator I got a glass bottle filled with well water. I put on a pair of white athletic socks and my leather slippers. I grabbed my red stocking cap as I went out the door otherwise I was still wearing my 'T' shirt and plaid flannel pajamas.

The Night Bus came at 2:00 o'clock sharp. When I climbed the steps into the bus and asked the raccoon bus driver to take me to the 'Place of Tanning', he turned the bill on his cap straight backwards, grabbed the steering-wheel firmly with both hands, leaned forward and coaxed the old bus out into the intersection where we stopped abruptly.

The bus began to sink slowly down into the pavement. It was as though we were in quicksand. The wet sand welled up around us covering all of the windows on the bus as air bubbles gurgled upward from beneath the bus. When the bus finally came to rest, the driver opened the folding doors in slow motion and a pale-purple cloud slowly tumbled into the bus. I got up out of my seat and moved into the cloud that seemed to me to be very dense. I along with everything else moved in super slow motion.

I stepped off of the bus into a small room filled with dense white fog. Everything was white. The fog was white. The walls were white. But, in the center of the small room was a round pad about thirty inches in diameter and maybe six or eight inches thick. I sat down on the pad as though I were going to meditate. First I tried to orient myself facing north but every direction faced north. Then, I tried to orient myself facing south, but every direction faced south. Next I tried to orient myself facing east, but every direction faced east. The last direction I sought was west. With that effort there was only one direction that was west and at that point the other cardinal directions all oriented themselves appropriately and a pathway appeared going in that direction with a single opening about two feet wide and six or seven feet high. I got up off of the circular pad and entered through the opening. As I entered, the space became a circular room with twenty-five vertical mirrors each one about twenty-eight inches wide and almost eight feet tall.

I had no idea, which if any of the mirrors, led out of this small circular, mirrored enclosure. At that moment, I pulled my red stocking cap down over my eyes covering my entire face. Then, only one of the mirrors remained. It faced southwest. I pushed that exit mirror open and found myself in a fog-filled place with no walls, no floor, no ceiling and only a single ornate wooden door straight in front of me. The door was massive. It was close to ten feet tall and six feet wide. It had no hinges, no doorknob and no keyhole. I had no idea how I could open it. When I touched it with my hand, my hand went right through the door. Then I stepped through the door. When I turned to the left a lush green landscape with green grass and trees and flowers appeared. I retrieved the bottle of well water that I had brought with me from home and attempted to pour it out onto the grass but only half of it came out but it remained intact as though we were in zero gravity or somehow frozen in time. I righted the bottle and the water went back inside in one piece as though it were jellied together.

When I turned to the right there was a doorway that

led into an oblong room with several horizontal tanning canisters in it. There were at least four on one side and four on the other side. I inspected each one of them by looking through a plastic window in the lid. In one of the tanning canisters was a young girl. I opened the lid and helped the young girl out of the chamber. She said that she was seeking the perfect tan. I told her that she already had a perfect tan and should be careful with those tanning machines because they could damage her skin. She went back into the tanning canister and as she closed the lid, she said, "Come back for me when you are ready." As I walked away, I recalled what the Source had said to me before I began this adventure. "You are ready."

So, I turned around and went back to retrieve the young girl from the tanning booth. But all of the tanning booths and the room itself had vanished. In their place was a single shower stall a little less than five feet in height with a huge shower head the same diameter as the shower stall itself spraying water down on the young girl creating a lot of steam.

I opened the door to the shower stall and extricated the young girl from within. She looked so familiar to me. I asked her if she were the girl that was frozen solid by liquid nitrogen two days ago. She said that she was. I told her that she had a beautiful tan. She said, "I just wanted to have young beautiful skin and an even tan."

I asked her if there were any place she wanted to go to. But, she didn't know where. So, I took her to Never Land because there was no way that I could leave her there in the 'Place of Tanning.'

When we arrived in Never Land, I introduced her to a young girl who had died in a terrible house fire. They gave each other a huge hug and they merged into one single person, one created from fire and ice.

Levantate Lazaro

I was asked by Lazaro's niece to look into his early demise. I located him in a small town with colorful buildings like you would find in Brazil or in Cajun country in Louisiana or even in Mexico. He was sitting in a very dark room with a single light overhead illuminating what he was doing. He was making figures of Jesus on a cross out of paper mache to be used at the Mardi Gras parade. He constructed them one at a time by hand like piñatas but they were more than twice the size of ordinary piñatas. They were hung on a wall after they were completed, to dry thoroughly. The first question I asked Lazaro was what happened to him. He told me that he did a line of cocaine and his blood pressure spiked and the circle of Willis in his brain blew out and he ended up dead and here in this place making paper mache replicas of Jesus for the Mardi Gras parade.

I asked him why he was making them but he didn't know. I asked him if he liked making them and he said no. I asked what else he did. He said that he has made one replica after another as long as he has been in this place. I asked him how long he had been here but he didn't know. I told him that this was his own personal Purgatory. He was here because he felt guilty for putting himself and his family through this whole ordeal from his premature death.

I told him that he would be free to leave this place, where he was sitting there making paper mache figures, as soon as he forgave himself for his past errors in judgment and poor decisions. I said to him, "Levantate Lazaro". Jesus loves you. Your niece loves you and they want you to forgive yourself so you can fly free.

Lazaro rose up from his chair and everything vanished. We were standing together in a field of golden California poppies. In the distance children could be seen playing a game like 'Kick the can'. We heard them singing, "All-ie... all-ie... all-ie ...ALL IN FREE.

Lazaro ran towards the children in the distance and disappeared.

Santori

Santori is not his real name but he passed away last week on a Sunday. I went looking for him Wednesday morning. I found him wondering around aimlessly in the desert. He didn't know where he was. He didn't know his own name. He was in a hurry because he said he needed to be somewhere and he was late but he had no idea where he was supposed to be going. At first I was walking with him and he was walking very fast. Eventually I got him calmed down enough that he sat down on a large rock. I convinced him to wait there for me until I returned later. It was obvious that only part of Santori was there. The rest of him had to be somewhere else.

Friday night when I checked in with the Source, He told me that I needed to find Santori now because he was in a bad situation. So, I went looking for the rest of him immediately. I finally found him tied to a wooden stake in absolute darkness being tormented by five or six 'Tormentors'. The Tormentors were temporarily repelled, by my light. Santori was unresponsive. I tried the potions and charms that I had with me but this was not a magic spell. This was not even Purgatory. We were in Hades. These tormentors were trying to turn Santori into a 'Tormentor,' like them. I needed help, and fast. So I contacted the Source and told him I was in over my head. At that moment a thin vertical sliver of light sliced through the darkness. That was our way out. I placed the mythical 'Celtic Cross' on Santori's forehead and he immediately came to life. We bolted through the slit of light making our escape from Hades.

The next challenge was to put Santori back together again. We went to the desert and found the other part of Santori still waiting for my return. He was sitting on the rock where I left him on Wednesday. I took both of them through the 'Door of No Returns'. They came out unified as one. From there I took Santori to the place of enlightenment to get him reunited with his deceased relatives. Jesus said, "He cannot pass over. He has lost his soul. You must first find his soul and return it to him." It's always something.

I ended up at the 'Cave of Lost Souls'. There was a giant monitor lizard guarding the entrance. I told the lizard who I was and that I had come to retrieve a lost soul. He withdrew and allowed me to enter the cave. Inside the cave I encountered a 'Whisp,' a tall ghostly woman dressed in a floor-length lavender gown. She floated about hovering a foot or so above the ground. The Whisp was the 'keeper of lost souls' but she had no idea which soul was which. It was up to me to find Santos. I summoned the lost soul of Santori. It lit up inside the glass flagon where it resided. I retrieved it and returned it to Santori where I poured it out onto him. From there we returned to the place of light where Jesus allowed him to pass over freely to the other side to rejoin his departed relatives.

Ghost at Grandma's House

I woke up this morning a little after 3:30 a.m. After I made a bathroom run, I was contemplating checking out the ghost at Grandmother's house when I saw the image of that ghost carrying a candle around looking for something in the dark. It was Grandmother herself. I fell asleep and woke up again an hour later in the dreamscape in the middle of a lucid dream. My wife escorted me across the street to a very large windowless structure with no doors. It was three or four stories high and took up the entire block. Its sides were sloped inward at an angle of five or six degrees. It was made entirely of ivory colored polished marble with rusty-brown striations. There was a small downward facing vent just above the sidewalk that was situated directly over a floor sink. Someone on the inside was pouring round, domed, disc-shaped ice cubes from inside the structure into the floor sink in the sidewalk. When I saw two hands protrude from the vent as they pushed the ice into the floor sink, I grabbed them and extracted a young lady with ivory-white waxy colored skin from the vent. At first she wouldn't tell me her name. But when I threatened to cut her head off with my sword, she told me that her name was Tess.

To me the structure looked like a super-sized mausoleum. Tess told me that it was "The Vault". She said that there was no way to get into the vault because there were no windows or doors leading into the vault. I asked her what was inside the vault but she wouldn't tell me. Upon closer scrutiny using the 'Wizard's powers of observation' I could see that Tess was in fact a mere skeleton. She volunteered that she was the 'Keeper of the Vault'. I used the magic sword to create an opening into the vault. The inside was vast and filled to the top with small clear pint size glass jars on shelves filled with different colored wisps of colored lights. I asked Tess what was in the jars and she admitted that they were 'Lost Souls' and she was in fact the keeper of those lost souls. I told her that I wanted the soul of Grandmother but she told me that she had no idea how to find any particular lost soul.

I was able to illuminate the soul of Grandmother that I was seeking by summoning her. The jar in which she resided glowed brightly. I grabbed it. Tess said that none of the souls in the vault were allowed to leave. I took it anyway and created an escape route through the thick marble walls with the magic sword.

When we arrived at Grandmother's House, I opened the glass jar and the ghost of Grandmother and her 'Lost Soul' united and were instantly transformed into the young, beautiful women that Grandmother had been when in her prime, by the power of her Grandmother's memories. She was dressed in a beautiful floor length ivory-colored silk, evening gown. I asked her where she wanted to go. She told me that she wanted to be reunited with her family. A beautiful, ornately decorated bridge appeared and I escorted her across the arched bridge into the other world where her family anxiously awaited their joyous reunion.

Mina

Mina is not her real name but she was the first homicide in Tucson, Arizona on Sunday January 5th 2020. Mina was stabbed to death by her younger brother in a heated argument at their home on South Holly Straw. Her brother is currently being held on a bond of $ 1 million.

Mina's cousin told me she was awakened by Mina,

her deceased cousin, a little after four o'clock in the morning, when Mina pulled the big toe on her right foot. I interpreted that event to be a plea from Mina for help. So, I went looking for Mina. I ended up in a very dark place with a very large alligator. My first thought was that Mina was in Purgatory and she had been turned into an alligator but when Mina began talking to me from inside of the alligator, I knew then that the alligator ate her. Getting an alligator to cough up someone they have eaten is not an easy thing to do but somehow, I managed to get it done.

    I took Mina into the 'Light'. Going into the light is the preferred process to go through especially if they have just been extricated from Purgatory, before they have completed their designated time there. As a Christian she was greeted, blessed and given safe passage into the realm of the dearly departed by Jesus. If she were Jewish she would have been greeted by Abraham. If she were a Muslim, she would have been greeted by the prophet Mohammed. If she were a Buddhist, she would be greeted by a Buddha. Once we had safe passage we were met by her Grandfather along with all of his deceased children and grandchildren.

Charmaine

    Charmaine is not her real name. She departed from this world at the age of seventy-four. Her sister asked if I could possibly provide her with any information regarding Charmaine's current situation and whereabouts.

Charmaine was unable to come to me when I summoned her, so I went to where she was. It was completely dark there, black and musty. I heard strange sounds coming from nearby. When I illuminated the space there was a giant toad the size of a number two washtub squatting next to me. When I tried to communicate with the toad I heard only gurgles and croaking. So I posed a series of questions to it and asked it to swallow in response to my yes or no questions. When toads swallow their eyelids blink and their eyeballs sink down into their heads squashing whatever prey they have just captured.

She intimated that she was Charmaine, that she had been bewitched and turned into a toad by her sister who cast a spell on her. I sprinkled fairy dust on her and she turned into a beautiful young lady in a floor length, white silk gown with long open sleeves and a tight circular neck.

Neither she nor I had any idea where we were but I told her I could take her to wherever she wished to go. Charmaine said that she didn't want to be dead. She wanted to go back to the world of the living. I explained to her what her options were. I could take her to be with her departed relatives or I could take her to see the 'Assignment Angel' to see what choices were available for immediate re-incarnation or I could take her to 'Never Land' where she would be safe until she decided what she wanted to do. I told her she couldn't go back to her home where she would just bother people and get herself into all sorts of trouble. She wanted to see what the 'Assignment Angle' had available so that is where I took her. The place for me is reminiscent of the Bonneville Salt Flats where they race cars and motorcycles. The 'Assignment Angel' always hates to see me coming. I can't imagine why.

I explained to the 'Assignment Angel' that Charmaine had recently died and had been bewitched by her sister and that she was anxious to return to the world of the living as soon as possible. The 'Assignment Angel' asked to see Charmaine's release papers from Purgatory. The 'Assignment Angel' then said that her sister was not a witch and no one put a spell on her. Charmaine had the opportunity to cross over when her departed relatives came to take her to the other side with them but Charmaine refused to go. She wanted to remain in the world of the living. Charmaine was sent to Purgatory where she was turned into a giant toad because she had a bad habit of telling stories her whole life. Charmaine had no documentation that she had completed her time in Purgatory and was released. The Assignment Angel wanted to know how Charmaine was able to get out of Purgatory. I explained to the Angel that I didn't know Charmaine was in Purgatory. I believed Charmaine when she said that her sister cast a spell on her. Dead people usually tell the truth.

The Angel showed us the unclaimed life scrolls she

had left in her bucket. There were only six. She told Charmaine that it was highly irregular to escape from Purgatory and there was no way to know what kind of life she would get if she chose to pick one of the six unclaimed scrolls. She definitely would not be go back into her own family. Her life would be of unknown gender, destination, and life's situations. Charmaine said that maybe it would be better to go to where her deceased relatives were.

The 'Assignment Angel' told her that the guards there wouldn't let her cross over without proof of release from Purgatory. She should have gone back with her departed relatives when they came for her after she died. We thanked the 'Angel for her assistance, then I took Charmaine to 'Never Land' where I introduced her to some of the residents there. I told her to not bother anyone. I would see what I could do about getting her some fake documents. I went to high school with kid named Tony. He might even be a relative of hers. He is long since dead now. He died of pancreatic cancer at too young an age. Tony always managed somehow to get us guys whatever we needed back then. He probably can get fake documents for Charmaine. If not, he probably knows someone who can.

I talked with Tony last night. He had established contact with Charmaine's relatives. Tony asked me to bring Charmaine over to where he was and someone from her family would be there to escort her safely back to where the rest of the family was located. I delivered Charmaine safely there. A tall man in a Stetson hat, wearing Levi's, a red plaid western shirt and cowboy boots spirited her away.

Jo-Jo

Born: March 19, 1975
Passed: March 22, 2019

Jo-Jo is not his real name.
Jo-Jo suffered from a fragmented personality. This created many serious issues for him during his lifetime.
Fragmented personalities also created many challenges for him in his afterlife.

Jo-Jo had three personality fragments:
The period from birth to age seventeen.
The period from seventeen until death.
The times he was under the influence of drugs or alcohol.

It was necessary to locate each of these three personality fragments and then to relocate them to separate safe places, before his recapitulation would become possible.
Recapitulation is the process of reviewing every event in one's life and then reconciling of each and every one of those events.
After each personality fragment had successfully completed their reconciliation, all three fragments

were united into a single personality by running them through the place of no returns.

Jo-Jo requested to reincarnate back into his family as the next available child without regard to health or gender.

Jo-Jo was taken to the 'Place of Reassignment' where the 'Reassignment Angel' presented him with a choice of three scrolls.

Jo-Jo chose one of the three scrolls, opened it and vanished.

Jo-Jo will return back into his Family in the guise of one of the next three children to be born into that Family.

Victoria

I became involved with Victoria at the request of someone close to her who was very concerned about her desperate situation.

Victoria was an eighteen year old healthy young woman who was swimming in her own pool, in her own back yard at around ten o' clock in the morning when she was discovered at the bottom of her pool by her parents who had moments before been talking with her. She was an expert swimmer and swam laps on a daily basis. She was a recent high school graduate who had received a full ride, four-year scholarship to pursue a degree in biochemistry at a prestigious eastern college. She was an outstanding musician and singer and a beautiful young lady. Her whole life lay ahead of her. She was in the hospital on life support after her drowning when I became involved with her.

I went looking for her and found her sitting on the edge of her swimming pool with her feet dangling in the water. She was still wearing her swimsuit. She was very distraught and disoriented. It took some time for her to calm down enough for me to begin to explain the situation to her. I told her that the situation did not look good but there were some things that we could attempt to do if she were willing to go through the trouble and accept the associated risks. When you are on life support your options are few and always fraught with substantial risk. In my personal opinion, there are many situations that are far worse than death.

Since neither she nor I had any idea what actually happened that created this situation, I suggested that we go back in time and attempt to use the butterfly effect to alter the outcome. I hoped we could shorten the time between the drowning and the rescue or better yet avoid the whole scenario all together. I told her to get on my back and hold on tight because I didn't want to loose her during the process of traveling back through time and not know where to find her. We arrived back at her home just before the event had taken place and she was swimming laps in the pool.

That was when things got really crazy. This thing, that I thought was a demon of some kind, zoomed down in a flash and took Victoria, who was right next to me leaving her body behind sinking down into the pool. Victoria was gone for at least fifteen or twenty minutes before she found her way back to the pool where I was waiting. I told her what happened and suggested that we try it again only this time I would be better prepared when the thing flashed down out of nowhere.

This time I was waiting holding the wizard's staff with its giant magical blue sapphire jewel on its top at the ready, like a batter waiting for a fast-ball on the outside of the plate. When this thing roared in I whacked it clean out of sight but when I turned around Victoria was gone leaving behind only her sinking body in the pool. It was some time before Victoria made it back to where we had been standing by the pool. I hoped my intervention had altered the outcome and we went to the hospital where I left her sitting on top of her body that was on life support and wished her the best. A few days later she was disconnected from life support. Our efforts had not been successful. The next time I saw Victoria she was exhausted from her futile efforts to re-connect with her own body which had been on life support.

I took her to 'The Place' where I hoped she could restore her energy levels and introduced her to the 'Source' who explained to her the futility of our efforts because of the irreversible brain damage that had occurred. I left them alone having their private and personal conversation. I assumed that she may have been shocked by a short circuit in a light or from touching a radio while still in the water but the Source insisted that it was her fate. When I asked about the demon that had zoomed in and taken her away, he said that it was one of the three Fates that had come for her.

I had heard of the myth of the Three Fates but I didn't believe that they actually existed. The Source even told me where I could find them. They were on an island known as the Island of the Three Fates. With this information I was able to locate the three sisters. The island was tiny and the three sisters were very large and very ugly. One had only a single eye in the middle of her forehead, another had three eyes and the third had five eyes. The one that had come for her was the one with five eyes. The Source told me that it was not possible for me to prevent that fate from taking another person when it was their time but what I had done when I whacked that Fate away was to make it impossible for my Fate to come for me when it was my time to be taken. With that I took Victoria home with me where she has remained. She declined to go to her own funeral. She said that was the past and she needed to move on. Victoria had cut a deal with the Source to reincarnate back into her own family as soon as a suitable baby would be born.

Ardyth Simpson

This morning early, a little after midnight I asked Victoria if she wanted to go with me to 'The Place'.

I was going to meditate there. She wanted to come with me so we had just situated ourselves there when the Source asked us to walk with him. He took us to a place that was green and lush with vegetation. We stopped at a split rail fence with what appeared to be a small farmhouse in the distance on the other side. He asked Victoria what she saw. She said that she didn't see anything. The Source asked me what I saw. On the other side of the fence there was a large field with tall grass and spring flowers of all kinds. Beyond the field there was a small, very small, wooden farmhouse. The Source told me to take Victoria over to the small house. Inside everything looked rather plain and antiquated. We looked all around the place and then left. When I turned around Victoria was gone.

    I asked the Source where she was. He told me that she was staying there. That was where she was re-incarnated on the 28th of October 1937 in Winona, Wisconsin. Her name was Ardyth Simpson. She was born at home in that farmhouse. She became a piano teacher and is still living somewhere. I asked the Source about Victoria wanting to be born back into her own family. He said that she was offered the chance to be her sister's child but she refused that opportunity and was re-assigned to this parallel life yet unfinished. I asked the Source why Victoria was unable to see what I saw. He said that she had already had her memory from her last existence wiped clean in preparation for her next life, besides she was not accustomed to time travel like I was and she was unable to process things from another time.

Thomas

Thomas was born June 25, 1971 and passed over on April 2, 2020.

Thomas was a patient of ours. He suffered from Cerebral Palsy and was severely debilitated. His mother sent a nice note to our office thanking us for the care we provided for him during the many years he was with us. I took it upon myself to check on him and see how he was doing.

I located him in a very dark place surrounded by demons. It was immediately evident to me that Thomas was in Purgatory. He was in a dimly illuminated space kneeling on the floor completely constrained by cords attached to every part of his body. Even his head was constrained in such a way that he couldn't move his mouth or even speak. I made my way over to him and told him that I was going to cut these cords that bound him, while keeping the demons at bay with the light-emitting disc I carry around my neck. Demons shun the light, any light. It causes them great pain. As I was cutting the cords I told Thomas that we had to get out of there. I told Thomas that I could take him anywhere he wanted to go. He needed to think about it and be ready to tell me where he wanted to go, as soon as I cut the cords that constrained him.

When I finished, I asked Thomas, where wanted to

go. He didn't know. He only said, "I want to be free." So, I took him to the 'Place of Assignment' and asked the 'Assignment Angel' if there were any lives available for Thomas. She pulled out a pair of 'Opera Spectacles' on each of his three choices. The Assignment Angel said, "The first choice is a life in the past in Australia. The second choice is in the present in Africa. The third choice is in the future as a girl."

Thomas said, "I just want to be free." He took the first scroll and vanished into the past in Australia. The Assignment Angel inspected me closely with her spectacles like I had fleas. I asked her what she was looking for. She said, "With these spectacles, I can see your soul."

Rankin

I was asked by an acquaintance to check out an old home she owned, for possible spirits. Old buildings and structures can sometimes harbor them. I checked the designated location at 2:00 o'clock this morning. There was a rough looking, grumpy old man sitting in an old wooden chair outside the door to this house. It appeared to be a back door or side door because it wasn't much of a door at all but I suppose it could have been the front door to a very old house.

It took me awhile to engage the old man in conversation. I tried several different approaches but I didn't get a response until I asked if he had been eating

French fries and dropped ketchup on his shirt. It clearly looked like an old bullet wound to the chest where his heart was located. That got him to reluctantly grumble a few words. I told him I could take him anywhere he wanted to go. He asked if I had a wagon. I told him I could get one. For every question I asked he had a curt, satirical answer. They were quite blunt, even humorous in a morbid sort of way. He certainly didn't have anything nice to say about the person residing there in that old house. He even accused him of stealing his hat, which back in his day was almost as bad as stealing your horse or your woman. As his story unfolded this is what I ascertained. He told me he was referred to by the name 'Rankin'.

He introduced me to his old dog 'Grover' and shared with me that he had a gal friend he called 'Sallie', who was by now long since dead and buried. I finally convinced him to leave with me when I told him he could bring his dog along with him. He went to get some stuff in the house and that was when he discovered his hat was missing. I heard him dragging something heavy across the floor through the house. It turned out to be a heavy old wooden box. He said it was filled with silver. I don't know if it was full of silver coins or bars of silver. He said that 'They' killed him for his silver but he never told them where he hid it. I convinced him that where we were going to see 'Sallie,' neither he nor she would have any use for it. Sallie already had everything she needed. I told him we needed to get a rope and I would hook it through his belt so he wouldn't get lost on the journey. He said he didn't have a belt so I tied one end of the rope around his waist and the other end around the dog's neck because Grover didn't have a collar.

The place where she was situated was lush and green with flowers and grass and trees everywhere. By the time we arrived at the attractive, well kept cottage where his gal friend lived, the man no longer appeared to be old but was now young and well dressed wearing a pair of light brown alligator boots, a new Stetson felt-hat and crisp, clean dress clothes that appeared to be freshly ironed. When the young lady answered the door and asked who I was, I introduced myself as Michael a traveling man. She told me her name was Margaret. When I said that 'Rankin' referred to her as his gal 'Sallie' she just gave him a dirty look and called him 'Joe'. Margaret invited all three of us in, Joe and me and the dog that was looking younger and in its prime. I looked all around inside before taking my leave as soon as it was possible.

The last action I took was to detonate a psychic explosive device in that old house, clearing out any stray ghosts, goblins or lingering spirits.

Emma

Last night I woke up and checked the time on the clock on my nightstand. It glowed in large red numerals, showing 3:59 a.m. I jumped out of bed and ran out to the driveway in front of our house. The Night Train was just pulling up and stopped right in front of me. This looked like the old steam engine on the Night Train but it seemed to be much larger than I remember, several times larger. The conductor got down from the first rail car. He was way bigger than he was before. He looked down at me and said, "Where you headed, kid?" I didn't say anything. He was a real giant. He said, "Let me help you up the steps. Just keep going until you find a seat that fits you."

The first passenger car on the train was lined on both sides of the isle with hard wooden bench-style seats. The backs of the seats were taller than I was. They were all empty of passengers. After that first car there were several sleeper cars. The doors on the compartments in the sleeper cars were all shut and locked tight. I couldn't read the names on the little white cards stuck in the card slots of each door. I finally came to the lounge car. There were booths on one side and a bar on the other side with a row of those tall bar stools anchored to the floor in front of the smooth mahogany counter top. The bartender sitting in the corner ignored me as I climbed up onto one of the bar stools upholstered in red leather. The stool seat swiveled around and around easily. My arms barely reached the bars counter-top.

Before too long a tall lady dressed in a grayish-green suit with a medium length skirt and matching hat sat down on the stool next to me. She was really pretty with her black hair, her blue, blue eyes and blood-red lipstick. Her manicured fingernails were painted to match her red lipstick.

She called me Mikey. She asked if I would like a soda. I didn't answer. She asked me if I liked root beer. I nodded affirmatively. She ordered a club soda for herself, on the rocks and a root beer for me. She asked if I liked ice cream. I didn't answer. She asked if I liked vanilla ice cream. I nodded yes. The bar tender gave her a club soda on the rocks and pushed a large root beer with a scoop of vanilla ice cream floating on top in front of me. It had two straws and an ice-tea spoon sticking out of it. I stirred it a bit and tried not to spill too much but my hands were quite small and didn't seem to work so well. The root beer float was really good. It was probably the best ice cream float I have ever had.

After the lady finished her club soda she moved very close to me and whispered in my ear that her name was Emma. She removed her gold locket from around her neck that was hanging on a long gold chain and bunched it up in the palm of her hand. She said,

"This contains all of my memories. Keep it safe for me until we meet again, in 1932." She left me with the small locket and my unfinished root beer float and she walked away.

I checked the dial on the clock. It was 4:10 a.m. I still held the small gold locket clutched in the palm of my hand. I was wondering what I should do with the locket. It was Father's Day. My wife would be waking up before too long. She would want to know what I was doing with the small gold locket. I knew she wouldn't understand so I decided to return it to Emma at her house in the year 1932.

I walked into her living room in 1932. It was a nice little house. The furniture looked old. Emma appeared to be about six years of age. She was taller than me. She had two ribbons in her hair. She was wearing a pretty party dress with black patent leather shoes and white socks rolled down at the top. She was very excited to see me. She said, "Mikey, you remembered." I gave her the locket. Emma put it around her neck and thanked me again. I was wearing a striped blue, yellow and white tee shirt and tan shorts. I was barefoot. She took me by my hand and we walked through the wall of her house and out into her beautiful yard filled with all kinds of flowers. It was summer time. I was barefoot. I never said a word. Emma talked incessantly. We sat down on a small blanket and had a picnic with tea and crackers. I never said a word. School was out for the summer but I still haven't started going to school yet. Well, maybe next year they will let me start.

Flanagan's Folly

I checked on Vestor Flanagan the next day after he killed the TV News Reporter and her cameraman. I for sure didn't want him coming into my house, so I went to where ever he was. I found him lying on his face in the grass near where he pulled his car off of the road and shot himself in the head with his 9mm Glock pistol when the police were coming for him.

When I aroused him he said that he had the worst headache and the worst bellyache that he ever had in his whole life. I left him there where I found him but I returned a few days later to check on him. I assumed that he would be in Hell somewhere but he was still in that same location. He was still complaining about his terrible headache. He said that he was starving and that he couldn't see out of one eye. One of his eyes had been eaten away by maggots and part of his face was missing.

I went back several more times to see if he had been taken away to Hell yet but each time more and more of him had been eaten away by mice and worms, exposing more and more of his skeleton. He lost the ability to see after his eyes were eaten away. He lost the ability to hear after his ears were eaten away. He lost the ability to speak after his tongue was eaten away. He still had a splitting headache and was starving twenty-four seven.

The last time I visited Vestor he was deaf and blind. He couldn't speak. He had flesh only remaining on his hands and feet and he still had his splitting headache and he was still starving to death. The only way for me to communicate with him was telepathically. His feet were jet black and his hands were snow white. The rest of him was just a light gray boney skeleton.

He spent every day and every night wondering aimlessly through the forest, constantly bumping into everything and constantly falling down.

I asked if he were sorry for what he had done. He

said that he would gladly do it all over again, even if it meant staying a thousand lifetimes in his current situation.

Perhaps he will remain 'The Boney Ghost of the Forest' for a thousand lifetimes to come.

Alison

I awoke this morning at 1:43 a.m. I had plenty of time to catch the night bus at 2:00 o'clock. I was concerned about the well being of Alison, the television news reporter who was recently killed along with her cameraman by Vestor Flanagan, so I thought I would take the Night Bus to where ever she was and check on her situation. Then on second thought, I decided that I should at least try to get her to come to where I was. That would be much easier for me.

I summoned Alison. She arrived in less than two minutes right beside my bed. That gave me fifteen minutes before the Night bus would arrive. I asked her how she was doing and told her I would take her anywhere she wanted to go. We could even take the Night Bus if she wanted to but she only had fifteen minutes to decide.

Alison told me she just wanted to go home and to be with her family. I reminded Alison that it would not be any fun because everyone was very sad and no one could see her and everyone would completely ignore her. Alison waited to the very last moment before she decided to take the Night Bus with me.

The bus was rounding the corner at the end of our street when we made it out to the curb in front of my house. On our way out of my bedroom, Alison asked who the old lady was there on the bed next to me. I told her that she was my wife. Alison wondered why I would be married to such an old lady. I asked Allison how old she thought I was. Her response surprised me. She thought I was maybe twenty-two. In the dreamscape dreamers and the deceased visualize you as they choose.

When the old Night Bus approached, Alison became very excited and animated and exclaimed, "A brand new school bus." The bus still looked really old and badly faded to me. Alison was completely shocked that the bus driver was a giant raccoon wearing a faded flannel shirt, dark pants and an old leather vest with his cap pulled down low over his eyes. I introduced them to each other and told Alison that Brad, the bus driver, would take her anywhere she wanted to go.

Alison asked Brad if he would take her on an adventure. So, he closed the doors securely and drove slowly straight ahead. We ran over several bumps in rapid succession before the bus came to a complete stop. Brad opened the doors to the bus and we stepped out onto a dirt path in the countryside surrounded by green grass, beautiful trees and flowers and birds singing all around us. It was springtime. Alison exclaimed, "This is where I grew up. This was my favorite place to play when I was a little girl." She looked to be six or seven years old. She was dressed in play clothes. I was six years old too. I was 'Lucky' the six-year old little boy that I once was. We held hands as we walked into the morning light and back into her childhood.

Selena

Selena Quintanilla-Perez was born April 16, 1971 in Lake Jackson, Texas; Selena died March 31, 1995 in Corpus Christi, Texas at 23 years of age, from a gun shot wound to the subclavian artery. She was known as the "Queen of Tejano Music". She ranks as one of the most influential Latin artists of all time. She performed in the genres of Tejano, Mexican Cumbia, Mariachi, Ranchera, Latin pop and R & B.

Sometimes when a person dies tragically and unexpectedly at an early age, they reincarnate in short order because they left so much unfinished business behind. The possibility that this might have happened in her case crossed my mind. That is what motivated me to see if that happened with Selena. I was surprised by what I discovered.

Selena was located in Purgatory chained on all fours to the floor. The chains were so short that she could neither stand nor sit but was forced to remain on her hands and knees with her head hanging down. What she did to deserve to be in this situation is unknown to me but I had no intention of leaving her in this situation.

After getting her attention by whispering in her ear, I informed her of her situation: She was in Purgatory, deceased and would remain there indefinitely until she successfully accomplished specific tasks. I explained to her that I would facilitate by providing the information she needed to accomplish those required tasks as quickly as possible.

Before I left I removed the chains from both hands and one ankle because her feet were spread far apart and that would not allow her to stand, sit or move around. Now she could sit or stand or lie down on the hard cement-like floor at will. I left one of her ankles secured because wandering around in Purgatory will get you in all kinds of trouble in no time at all. Next I procured a giant red, bell pepper-like thing, cleaned out the insides and placed it around her to protect her from the demons that dwell there in Purgatory. I told Selena to rest and recuperate. I said I would return on the morrow, when we could begin the process of extricating her from Purgatory.

When I returned she was sitting with her knees pulled up and her head resting down on them. Her arms were wrapped around in front of her legs. I told her she needed to forgive all of her real and imagined insults and injuries as well as forgiving herself for all the bad things that she had done as well as things left undone, before she would be able to leave this place. Seemingly in no time a shaft of light splintered the darkness and shown down on her from above. It enlarged to include me as well and we were lifted up and floated out of purgatory by some mystical power.

From there I took Selena to 'Never Land', where I left her in good hands. I advised her caretaker that she needed to rest and begin the arduous task of recapitulation, which would take as long as it took. There is no way to predict how long that process will ultimately take. After that step is complete we can take her to the place of re-assignment where she can begin again in a new life in a different time and different place as a different character.

She is making good progress after a week or so. Hopefully she will be ready to move on to her next life soon. I check on her every few days or so. When she had recuperated adequately I left her in front of a magical fire that requires no additional wood it just keeps burning and burning like a gas log but it is fueled by real wood not gas. I wrapped her in a blanket and left her there to ponder upon the challenges of her situation. I thought that working through the details of her untimely death and her murder by one of her assistants would be very problematic but hopefully that would be the last and greatest obstacle preventing her from moving on. As it turned out, there was an even greater obstacle than that, which surprised me.

We talked through each of her difficult challenges. After her conflicts and murder had been worked through she revealed an even greater challenge for her to overcome. She told me that her father drove her relentlessly like a dog. She always wanted to believe that her father did everything in her best interest but finally realized that he was just using her for his own gratification. He wanted fame and fortune at any cost, no matter the pain and anguish that she was forced to endure.

Deep Blue Sea

Amy passed away two weeks ago. I think fifty-seven years old is too young to die. I went looking for her a couple of days later. I found her wandering along the side of a road in the middle of the night disoriented and very confused. I picked her up and took her home with me to give her a chance to recover. I asked Amy if she wanted to attend her own funeral on Saturday but advised her that everyone there would be immensely saddened and greatly depressed. She would be totally ignored by absolutely everyone. She decided that she would skip her own funeral.

I had not seen Amy for three days so I decided to check on her last night. I found her hanging from some strange looking transparent flesh-like tentacle wrapped around her wrists with her arms extended outward behind her back. She was dangling there suspended in mid-air. It looked to be horribly painful for her. The place had no floor and no walls. The fleshy tentacle just ended about fifteen feet above her head. I had no idea how she ended up in this situation but I knew that I had to do something to get her out of her current predicament.

I checked with the Facilitator, and then with Sabatini, the Traveler's Buddha. Neither of them had ever seen anything like this before and had no idea how to remedy the situation. I knew I would have to go to the big guns if I were going to deal with this situation successfully. I summoned Ganesh, the Elephant God and Hanuman, the Monkey God. One appeared on one side of Amy and the other appeared on her other side. They stared up at the end of the tentacle, which ended in the middle of nowhere. They didn't know what to do with the situation either.

Next I rose above the place where the tentacle abruptly ended and there was nothing so I summoned Shiva the God of destruction. He appeared but said that he didn't know what to do with the situation. I summoned Krishna. He appeared and explained to me that this was a trap set for me by the Devil. Amy was used as the bait to lure me there. If I cut the fleshy tentacle, which suspended Amy, the trap would be tripped and it would collapse in on me and crush my consciousness. If I left Amy there she would become increasingly angry and eventually she would be transformed into some sort of a demon from her unending pain and anguish. I had no idea what I could do to free Amy. I recalled a saying my mother used when she was in an untenable quandary when I was a little kid. I never really understood what it meant.

She would say, "Between the Devil and the deep blue sea." Since I needed to free Amy without cutting the dangling tentacle I summoned the Deep Blue Sea and it began pouring into the waiting trap. The clear cold water of the Deep Blue Sea revived Amy and floated her upwards freeing her entangled wrists. The tentacle shriveled up and disappeared when the pure cold seawater touched it. We were freed from the trap set for me by the Devil.

Now after all these years, I finally understand what my mother was trying to say when she would tell me that she was caught 'Between the Devil and the Deep Blue Sea.'

Chicago

No sooner had I rescued Amy than she told me she was going to catch the three o'clock to Chicago. I advised her to be careful. She said that she would be fine. Two days later I checked on her. I found her hanging from the ceiling with a heavy hemp rope tied around her wrists. Her back was covered with raised, red whelps. Someone or something had been beating her with a rope or whip.

I looked all around the dark dungeon and saw an ugly creature hunched in the corner still holding a long leather lash in his left hand. He looked like a gargoyle to me. I summoned Constantine from the distant past. He burst onto the scene and the gargoyle was swiftly decapitated. Once again I rescued Amy and brought her back to my house. I reminded her that there are a lot of really bad things a person can run into when they are no longer living but deceased. And, once again I offered to escort Amy to anywhere or any when that she wanted to go. But Amy has yet to make up her mind. So in the mean time I guess she will be hanging around my house.

I woke up and checked the clock. It showed 2:01 a.m. in large red numerals. I asked Amy if she wanted to go somewhere on the Night Bus. She said yes so we hurried out to the front of the house where the Night Bus stood waiting for us with its doors swung open wide. Brad asked her where she wanted to go. Amy said, "Take me home, I wanna go home."

Brad the raccoon bus driver took the first left and then another left. I assumed we were heading for her house located here in Tucson where she and her husband have raised their four daughters but I was mistaken.

We stopped somewhere in the distant past in an unknown place for me. When Amy stepped off of the bus she was a seven year-old little girl. She met her mom and dad there from fifty years ago. She introduced me to her family and told them I was 'Mikey'. I was a little kid just like her.

Amy said to me as she walked away together with her family, "Home is where your heart is" then, they all disappeared.

Animal Shelter

Last night while I was talking with the Source I asked him what activity I should concentrate on for the moment. The Source said that I needed to go and check on Amy. I assumed that I was finished with that project but I went looking for Amy as he suggested. I decided to take the Night Bus when it came by at 2:00 o'clock in the morning. When I got on board I asked Brad, the raccoon bus driver, what he was hauling tonight and he said, "Injured elephants". I looked around the bus and it was indeed filled with injured elephants. I told the bus driver that I needed a ride to wherever Amy was. He dropped me off after a few minutes ride.

I found myself in an animal shelter where every kind of injured animal you could imagine were all around me with every injury they could possibly have sustained. Amy was standing at the far end of the treatment and recovery facility diligently treating all of these many sick and injured animals.

Apparently this was her calling. Apparently this was her heaven. This was where she wanted to spend her eternity helping these sick and injured animals to recover.

Two Gold Coins

I woke up a little after three in the morning. One of our two Cardigan Welsh Corgis was panting. The air conditioner was on and the house was cool. There was no reason for the dog to be panting like she was. Over in the corner next to her dog bed there was a tall skinny man standing next to her. He was hunched over like he had a bad back. He was wearing tight pants that ended just below the knee. His leather shoes were black with a single buckle on them. His stockings were very dark in color. He wore a long sleeve shirt with a fancy collar and a dress coat with tails and open at the front. He moved towards me with his left hand extended. I had no idea as to who he might be or what he wanted from me.

I extended my left hand towards him with the palm facing upward. He placed two gold coins in my hand. I asked him what they were for. He said that one of the coins had the tails side facing upward and the other coin had the heads side facing up. That way I would always be prepared for whichever side landed up in a game of chance. I thanked him for the two gold coins and asked him who he was and what brought him to my bedroom in the middle of the night.

He told me that his name was Silverstein, Joseph Silverstein and he was from Vienna, Austria. He said that he was the same age that I was and he had come from the year 1703. When I asked him again why he had visited me, he said that he was a past incarnation of myself and he wanted me to be prepared for whatever chance brought my way. I thanked him once again and he disappeared.

About half an hour later I thought I should try to visit

him in his year of 1703. When I arrived there where he was, he was in what we might call an alley. Three thugs were attempting to rob him at knifepoint. I transformed myself into a terrible beast and the three of them quickly fled as fast as they could. He was grateful for the rescue but wanted to know how I managed to pull off that transformation. I told him it was something that I learned along the way and I left it at that. I thanked him once again for the two gold coins. They may come in handy someday since life itself is really just a game of chance.

Blue Moon Two

A Blue Moon is the second full moon that occurs in a single month. This happens occasionally. It is unusual when there is more than one Blue Moon in a specific year. In the year 2018 there was a Blue moon in January and another one again in March. The last time there were two Blue Moons in a single year was 1999 and the next time that happens will be in the year 2037. The second full moon this year in March is supposed to come at 7:09 p.m. this evening on the 31st of March.

Last night when I went to 'The Place' to recharge my energy supply at 1:15 in the morning, the Source wanted me to go to where the Magic Crows were gathering for their monthly Full Moon meeting. I told the Source that I didn't know where the meeting was going to be held and besides that, the full moon wasn't supposed to be until this evening.

The Source said that he would take me there to where the Magic Crows were gathering in the Urals where it was already the full moon. He also told me that I would have to go as pure awareness so that I would be difficult for the Magic Crows to detect.

When I arrived I located the Spanish Crow. She is the only crow that still communicates with me. I whispered in her ear, "I am here, I am here, can you hear me?"

She said, "Where are you?"

I answered, "I am near. I am pure awareness. Where are we? Are we in the Ural Mountains in Russia? What year is it anyway?"

She said, "Quiet the other crows are looking at me. It is in the year 1917."

I watched quietly from atop the Spanish Crow's head as the monthly full moon gathering proceeded. I recognized the old crow wearing his pince-nez spectacles that brought their meeting to order. He said that for the first time their International 'Order of Magical Crows' had experienced a decline in their membership. No wonder, for sorcerers are a dying breed and sorcery is a dying art.

When I returned to 'The Place' to recharge once again, the Source told me that I needed to go see the 'Buddha on the Mountain'. So, I went there. When I entered the cave the Buddha asked me to come on his side of the fire-pit. Usually I sit on the opposite side of the pit facing the Buddha with the fire in between us. So I went to his side of the fire-pit and started to sit down facing the fire, which I always do. The Buddha asked me to sit facing him instead of the fire, so I did. I sat down with my legs crossed as though I were preparing to meditate. As I sat there facing the Buddha, I began to slowly rise up off of the ground until I was suspended in mid-air at the same level the Buddha was sitting in his chiseled-out alcove. Then I began to move forward towards him until we merged into one being and I was looking out of the alcove at the fire-pit through his eyes.

A young boy about six years old entered the cave and approached me. He had dark hair and dark eyes. He was neither of light complexion nor dark complexion. He hugged me around the neck and said, "Thank you for releasing me so that I can begin my next life."

When I returned home I asked the Source what that experience was all about. He told me that I had been the 'Buddha on the Mountain' in another lifetime and that the boy was key to understanding this puzzle. I responded, "That must be why I am so weird." The Source said, "No, that is why you are capable of doing all the many things that others can never do."

Roberto Islas

The Source had said that the boy was key to my understanding the situation, so I went looking for him wherever that might end up being. Eventually I found him. He appeared to be a little bit older now, perhaps seven years of age. When I located him he was out in the countryside away from any roads or houses or other people. I asked him what his name was and he said Robert. I asked where he was born. He said Uruguay. I asked if he spoke Spanish. He said yes but we were communicating in English. Robert told me that he spoke both Spanish and English and when asked he told me that his last name was Islas and that he answered to both Robert or to Roberto.

I asked him when he was born. He said on the seventh day of the seventh month of the seventh year. That would make it on July seventh but the specific year was still in question. Robert told me he was born during the seventh year of his parent's marriage.

Joseph Silverstein

The Source told me more than one time that I needed to round up all of the characters from my alternate life experiences and to make a personal connection with each of them before I would be able to move on. Joseph Silverstein was one of the very last ones. When I found him he was very old. I explained to him what the situation was and he agreed to go with me through the "Door of No Return". We entered together but only I exited on the other side. I reached into my pocket and there were the two gold coins Joseph Silverstein had given me years ago. As I walked down the cobblestone road towards town I came upon several beggar children. I gave them the two gold coins for I knew that I would have had no use for them where I was going.

As I continued down the road I grew younger and younger. My clothing slowly changed. I ended up dressed as Tom Sawyer with a fishing pole over my shoulder and a can of worms in my hand. I had no shoes or shirt on, just a ratty old straw hat and old overalls that were two sizes too small. As I approached the river a large number of young women gathered around me. They were all of the many females that had accompanied me during my past lives. They all cried out for me to join them in the river.

As they entered the river they all were transformed into beautiful gold fish. Instead of walking into the river as they did, I walked above the surface of the water and when I reached the other side the landscape was totally barren. Nothing existed on the other side. I turned and looked back over the river and it had turned to sand. There was nothing but sand, the 'sands of time' as far as the eye could see.

When I stepped onto the land on the other side of the river it was transformed into the beautiful countryside where I met Robert Islas before. He was standing there alone. He asked, "Who are you, mister?" I said, "I don't know."

Robert said to me, "You see too much and know too little. I on the other hand know too much and see too little. Together we can see enough and know enough to get the job done."

Robert Islas said, "Together you can know more and

I can see more." We held hands and he took me to where there was what looked like a bird's bath and he said for me to drink from it. I did so and a pathway appeared behind him. He said for us to go down the path together because it was a path that he could not see. We walked down the path holding hands and facing each other. He walked backwards and I walked forwards until we came to a fork in the road. He turned around and said that he could now see the path that diverged to the left but not the path that continued to the right.

Robert turned around and walked away down the pathway to the left and I turned and walked down the pathway to the right. It continued until it opened up into a clearing. The Source was waiting for me there. He said, "I see you finally made it." He asked me to walk with him. As we walked he said, "This is the 'Place of Knowing'. Here is where you come whenever you need to know something."

Jonathan

Jonathan passed unexpectedly a week ago. His untimely death concerned me. I wanted to check on him and see how he was managing his new situation. I had no idea where he was but I felt it would be less problematic for him if I went to where he was instead of having him come to where I was. When I located him he was walking with another man who was wearing a brown, hooded, floor length cloak. Jonathan was wearing casual clothes and was carrying a backpack. They were walking briskly along a dirt pathway in the middle of a desert wilderness. I walked behind them having difficulty keeping up with their rapid pace. I attempted to communicate with Jonathan several times to no avail, before I tapped him on the shoulder to get his attention. I asked where they were going and why they were walking so fast. He said that they were in a hurry because they were late. But he never told me why he was late or where he was headed. When I tapped the other man on his shoulder to get his attention, he vanished. I asked Jonathan what the fellow traveler's name was and he said, "Job".

    I asked Jonathan if he wanted to take a break and we sat down on a rock near the trail we were walking on. There was a stream not too far down the hill below us and so I asked him if he saw the stream or small river. He said that he did and then I asked what he was carrying in his backpack. He said that he didn't know what was in the backpack. I asked if he knew where he was but he didn't know. I asked how long it had been since he last ate and he didn't remember. I asked what the last thing he ate was and after much deliberation he said that he had eaten chicken but that it didn't agree with his stomach and that was the last thing he remembered. He didn't know what day it was or where he was going or why he was in such a hurry. I suggested that he look inside of his backpack and see what he was carrying.

    He opened it up and the first thing he removed from

the backpack was a large egg. It wasn't a chicken egg because it was much larger than a chicken egg. It was so large that I thought it could be a duck egg or maybe even a goose egg. The second thing he removed was a round rock slightly larger than the egg. The third thing he removed from his backpack was a baseball. The next thing was a stick a little over a foot in length and about ¾ of an inch in diameter. The last thing he removed was a hand full of feathers. They weren't chicken feathers but gray feathers from a pigeon or a morning dove. We talked at length about what those things represented in general and to him specifically.

Jonathan struggled to give meaning to those items he had been carrying in his backpack. I felt they were critical for him to understanding his current situation. For me the egg represented a new beginning, like Easter and spring represents rebirth and new life. The rock represents something hard, something heavy and something enduring like life and death itself. Baseball represents a game, the game of life. A stick is part of a tree that was once part of a living tree but is now no longer alive. The stick represents his piece of the tree of life and part of his own family tree. Dove feathers represent peace and hope but the dove itself is now gone. The person who accompanied him on his journey through the wilderness was Job, a biblical prophet. The wilderness itself also alludes to the biblical journey of redemption, and the river down below where we were sitting was in fact the river Jordan. I explained this to Jonathan and suggested that he toss all those things he was carrying into the river and then get on with it.

He wanted me to toss the items into the river but I told him that this was his journey and his task not mine. Jonathan said that he liked the egg and wanted to toss it into the river last of all.

First he tossed the rock into the river as he stood on an outcropping. The stone sank to the bottom of the stream and was transformed into gold. The second thing he tossed into the water was the baseball. It turned into a small wooden boat and drifted away down the river. I asked which way it drifted, to the right with the current or to the left against the current. He said that it drifted with the current down the river to the right. I asked him to look up the river to the left and tell me what he saw. He saw that same little wooden boat drifting towards him from his left, and passing by heading to his right. Every minute or so, the boat would drift by once again continuing on its journey. Next he dropped the stick into the water. It sank straight to the bottom as if it were made of iron. After the stick Jonathan dumped the pile of feathers into the river and the river turned a beautiful blue like the color of a tropical sea. Before he dropped the egg into the water he threw his backpack into the river. It unraveled and became a bundle of threads waving in the current stretching off into the distance attached to the spot where the backpack entered the river. The last thing he tossed into the river was the oversized egg. It sank immediately to the bottom of the river and all of the things he had tossed into the river began to coalesce around the egg and up out of the water popped a white swan with its prominent black bill. It grew larger and larger as Jonathan shrank smaller and smaller. When the swan was full size Jonathan was as small as a hamster. I picked him up, dunked into the river Jordan and placed him on the back of the swan. I told him to hold onto the swan's neck by wrapping his arms and legs around the swan's neck. They flew away together. The magical white swan transported Jonathan off to begin his next life.

My assessment was that this was his purgatory. There is no way to know how long Jonathan would have wandered in the desert wilderness before he figured out that he was deceased and how to extricate himself from this place. It could have been a very long time. I in essence short-circuited his stay here in Purgatory. I liked Jonathan. He was a good man.

Jeanie

Kitty called. It was late in the afternoon. Dinner was almost ready. I was surprised to see the name 'Kitty,' appear on the telephone screen. We hadn't heard from her for fifteen years. We were in the military together for three and a half years, stationed in North Dakota. Her husband and I arrived on base in December a few days apart, as second lieutenants. We were assigned to the Strategic Air Command for ballistic missile duty. They became our surrogate family. They had two children while stationed there. We had one child born in between their two children. We kept in contact with them for many years but as time passed things changed and we eventually lost contact.

Kitty said she called because she came across some old papers, some poems and children's stories I wrote forty years ago and wanted to know if she should return them. But, that didn't turn out to be the real reason for her call. Her family is pretty much all gone now. Her fifty-one year old daughter, who was in perfect health, returned from a trip by air in February, got sick from the Corona virus and passed away just days later. Kitty had been struggling with the loss of her only daughter since then. That was six weeks ago. She needed to talk with someone who would understand. She needed to share with family. We were her surrogate family. Kitty talked for a long while with my wife. I think that helped her a lot. I talked for a short time with her. It left me wondering if there might be something else I could do in her time of crisis. So, I went in search of her daughter Jeanie.

I ended up in Hades. It was completely dark. Not dark, dark but totally without any light what so ever. It had taken me many trips to Hades in the past, before I finally mastered the skill of seeing without any light. Above Hades is Purgatory. There are all of these cylinders that open into Hades, which is the beginning of Purgatory. I located the cylinder where Jeanie was located. She was on her knees leaning over a reflecting pool wearing a Native American Indian dress made of buckskin. It took several attempts before I was able to get her to look away from her own reflection. She had the face of a monster. I don't have any idea why she was in Purgatory nor do I know why she had the face of a monster. I was there to rescue her from her demons, real or imagined. The top of the cylinder she was located in was wide open so, we escaped through that opening and went to where the Assignment Angel is located in the place of re-assignment. The Assignment Angel hates to see me coming. It seems I am always breaking the rules. We must have caught the Angel in a good mood, for she gave Jeanie a scroll for her new life without any hassle. It must have been because of the Corona Virus and Jeanie's early demise at the early age fifty-one.

Ram

Ram passed away yesterday. He had been on a ventilator in a coma for twenty-nine days after contracting the Corona virus. I chose to intervene on his behalf because I knew him, I respected him and he was in my mind, part of a large extended 'family circle'. I went looking for him last night a little after midnight.

When I found him, he was being taken away to somewhere by a pair of demons, that were about five feet tall. They reminded me of gremlins but were much larger, more muscular and had grotesque monster faces like Hindu demons. I took out my magical half-sword and threatened to chop their heads off if they didn't release him. It was immediately apparent to me that he wasn't all there. I took him to a safe place and went looking for the rest of him. I found that other part of him at home in his house. If he stayed there he would become a ghost and cause nothing but trouble for everyone so I took that part of him to where the other part was located. The two separate personality fragments were not conjoining so I took them through the 'Door of no Returns' where they were re-united and became one personality again. I asked Ram where he wanted to go, then took him to be re-united with his deceased family. We were greeted by a group of several people. A short little chubby gray-haired women hugged him. Then they departed back beyond the pale all together. I assume that she was his mother.

Later I went to the Island of Vishnu. I wanted to know if the pair of monsters was Hindu demons. I went to the small fire pit which was filled with glowing embers, sat down in front of it and sprinkled a hand full of tiny dried leaves of some kind that were nearby and waited for the Gods to arrive. First came Hanuman, Shiva, then Ganesh and Janaki. Last of all came Krishna. When they were all assembled Krishna said that my intervention had angered the Hindu Gods that were taking Ram to be punished for his arrogance. The young boy 'Innocence' was going to accompany me to help protect me from the angry Gods. The Goddess Janaki placed a red bindi on my forehead as a sign of reverence.

For some reason I began 'Thumping' on the cherry

headboard on our bed. It produced a strange sound. I instinctively knew the Hindu Gods were stirring. I knew this sound, this rhythm, was a warning to them to stay at bay. It was 4:04 a.m. when I looked at the clock. I rushed outside. The night train was there waiting. The conductor said they had been waiting for me. He told me I was to go from car to car touching every occupant. I jumped on the train. It was composed of only cattle cars. In the past it had always been only passenger cars. These cars were obviously cattle cars but they were connected just like passenger cars with doors and passageways between each car.

I moved from car to car touching each cow on the forehead, cow on the left, cow on the right, cow on the left, all facing me as I passed. There were eleven cows lined up in each of seven cattle cars. The last car was very, very long. There were so many cows, that I lost count. I think between ninety and ninety-nine. At the very end was an enlarged space with a single Hindu Deity sitting cross-leg on a throne. It was Surabhi consort to Brahma. She touched me on my forehead and said, "Thank you for blessing the elven cows in the seven cars which each represented seven manifestations of the eleven Rudras." Manyu, Manu, Mahmasa, Mahan, Siva, Rtudhvaja, Urgraretas, Bhava, Kama, Vamadeva and Dhrtavrata.

I returned the next night to the Island of Vishnu to ask Krishna if he knew the two demons that were dragging Ram away. He summoned them to the fire pit, and introducing them to me as the twin Gods Asvini

Kumaras, the twin Gods of health and medicine. They looked like demons to me. At that, they transformed themselves into their human forms. I also asked Krishna about the elongated cattle car with almost a hundred cows in it. He said that the super-size cattle car represented the totality of human kind and the ninety-nine cows represented the true Hindu believers.

We all bowed to each other saying: Namaste… Namaste…Namaste

Bus of No Return

I began working systematically on gathering experience within the fourth attention last week. My first attempt was while preparing to board the Night Train at 4:00 o'clock in the morning. When the conductor shouted "All aboard" and asked me where I needed to go, I told him, "The fourth attention." He told me to go up to the coal car and climb inside it through the small door that the fireman used to shovel coal into the train's boiler. I followed his instructions, got inside of the coal car and closed the door behind me. I woke up several hours later and remembered nothing. The next night when I boarded the Night Bus at 2:00 o'clock in the morning I noticed that the bus that was normally empty of passengers was completely filled with very transparent people, just barely discernable to my eyes. When I asked Brad the bus driver about these barely visible transparent passengers, he told me that they had always been there.

That night I had a coherent dream that lasted over an hour. A coherent dream is a continuous, uninterrupted, lucid dream that unfolds at a normal rate of speed. The next night I had a coherent dream that lasted for three hours. Another oddity was that I had no difficulty remembering the dreams in great detail and I was completely rested as though I had slept soundly, undisturbed throughout the entire night. That gave me my first inkling as to how a master could possibly never sleep but be totally awake and totally aware and totally asleep at the same time. The next night when I got on the Night Train the engineer met me instead of the conductor and told me to get into the firebox of the boiler. I climbed into the raging flames in the firebox but only remember that it was really hot in there.

The next night I again ventured into the fourth attention via the Night Bus. This time the passengers appeared more real and less transparent but none of them seemed to move a single muscle. On this trip I ended up standing at a long wooden worktable where I mixed white powder, resembling unbleached flour, with some crystalline substance that I thought might be salt and a clear liquid that appeared to be water, until the mixture resembled bread dough. Next I placed this dough into a contraption like an elaborate Play Dough machine and squeezed the dough until it disappeared from the machine.

The following evening when I boarded the Night Train all of the passengers appeared to be complete like real people. All of the seats on the bus were occupied. One of the passengers got up from his seat so that I would have a place to sit down. As he passed by me on my way in, he left the Night Bus at the same time. He was a large young man about 6 feet 5 inches tall with blond hair that was almost shoulder length and blue, blue eyes. He was obviously of northern European decent.

I asked the bus driver who the big guy was and Brad told me that his name was William Tate and that he was born in 1689 in what would someday become Sweden. He journeyed to America in 1721 at the age of 32. He would eventually make his way to what is now known as Tennessee. He also told me that all of the passengers on this bus were unable to ever return, to ever re-incarnate, unless someone like me created a new life for them as I had done when I forced that doughy material through the mold in the machine. That act created William Tate and gave him the opportunity to have another life.

It was another opportunity for his lost soul as a passenger on the 'BUS OF NO RETURN'.

Magic Mountain

Last night, I went out early to catch the Night bus. When I climbed on board, every one of the forty-seven passengers were celebrating and making all kinds of noise. I asked all of them if they wanted an opportunity to have another life experience. They were so excited about this possibility they all urged me to try to pull it off. The approach I had in mind, seemed on the surface to have some merit, so I asked Brad the bus driver, to take us to Magic Mountain. It is a small mountain located on an Indian reservation in South Dakota. I think it is on, or near the Pine Ridge Oglala Lakota Community.

Magic Mountain is supposed to contain a portal to another reality. When Brad let us off near the face of its towering cliffs, I told everyone to follow me in single file and pretend that I was a Pied Piper. I told them that we were going to walk right into the side of the mountain but if they hesitated or doubted for a single moment, they could loose this opportunity to have another chance at life.

As the passengers from the 'Bus of No Return' emerged from the other side of the mountain, I counted them carefully in hopes that most of them had made it through the solid granite mountainside. To my surprise, all forty-seven of the passengers survived their passage through the mountain. They all emerged fully dressed in authentic Native Indian buckskin attire. They were now newly minted Lakota. I summoned a herd of horses for them to ride. Forty-eight horses thundered towards us, all were paints except the lead stallion, which was cloud white. Each Lakota mounted a steed and they all galloped off towards the west, into the setting sun. The one remaining horse was the snow-white stallion. He slowly approached me, closer and closer, until our noses touched. I leaped onto his powerful shoulders and we whirled and raced eastward towards the new day that would accompany the rising sun.

While the passengers from the 'Bus of No Return' were transformed into fully clothed Native American Lakota Indians and rode west on their paint ponies, I became pale white and rode off in the opposite direction on this white stallion, completely unclothed, like Lady Godiva. We traveled together for some time before I finally discovered the name of this beautiful white stallion. His name was Destiny.

In our travels together, we came upon a crude wooden table. Upon the table were three separate bundles, roughly wrapped in crude white paper. Each package had a different word printed on it in large black upper case letters. The three packages were labeled: Dentistry, Destiny and Death. Since the name of the horse was Destiny, I chose that package. I had no interest in Death or Dentistry, so the remaining two packages slowly faded and disappeared. As I unraveled the bundled package, the first thing that appeared was a single white Lily of the Valley flower. The next item to appear, as I continued to unravel the bundle, was a single white rose. The third item was a long white frilly feather from some kind of exotic bird. The fourth item was a rectangular piece of white linen, slightly larger than two large cloth table napkins combined end to end. I rolled up the linen cloth along its short axis and placed it around my head like an Indian headband. Then, I placed the Lily into the band near my left ear, the rose near my right ear, and the feather in the very back of my head. The last item in the package, was a good size book, 12" X 16". It was bound in pure white leather, with a gold cross, emblazoned on its center. I assumed that this book must surely be a large Christian Bible.

I opened the thick cover of the book embossed with its gold cross. Inside was an opening into a pastel-colored springtime scene from some beautiful magical place. Destiny and I passed through this narrow opening and emerged into another world filled with light, beautiful flowers, green grass and lush trees. On the right side of the unpaved pathway stood a tall man with silver gray hair who was dressed in a long flowing, white, floor-length robe. He welcomed us into his lovely world. He explained that he was showing me, my destiny. The light grew brighter, and more abundant, as we moved deeper into my future. When it became abundantly clear to me that this gentleman was showing me where I might be headed after I was already deceased, I interrupted his train of thought by asking him who he was. When he told me that he was Father Time, I knew it was time for us to backtrack and get out of there. We made our way back the way we had just come, leaving Father Time standing there, at the last portal before the afterlife and exited the large leather bound book.

I held it in my hands for some while, before once again opening the cover with its golden cross. This time, there was another page beneath the thick white leather bound cover. On it were the words:

Lucid Journey
Followed by:
A Two-Year Odyssey

As I thumbed through more pages, I knew that it was my destiny to complete this book.

Subsequently, I changed the name from Lucid Journey to:

"Coincidental Journey"
A Two Year Odyssey

It could always be changed back to "Lucid Journey" at the time of first publication.

The Spinnaker & the Imp

Last night at 9:00 o'clock my wife asked me to check the front door before we went to sleep. When I checked, the outside half door was wide open and the regular door was ajar. We never leave the doors like that.

When I went back to our bedroom she said that there was something there. I asked where and she said right next to her on the bed. She told me that when I went to check on the front door, she felt a breeze like the air conditioner had come on but it had not and then something touched her and it was still there right next to her.

It took me a while to figure out what was there and why. This is what I discovered: A small creature less than two feet tall was sitting on my wife's side. It looked a little like a Gremlin with large pointed ears, big eyes and a huge mouth filled with pointy teeth. It was slight of build and covered with light brown hair. When I observed it through my rose-colored glasses its appearance changed to a small black-skinned boy wearing a carved, black, African, wooden mask. When I looked at it again through the double-lensed, pince-nez glasses the creature was still black but its black mask had become a ferocious black face. When I viewed the creature's reflection in the 'Sword of Truth' the image was that of a pug-nosed little Anglo boy. First I asked it to get off of my wife and to come over to my side of the bed. It obliged my request and stood on the floor next to me staring at me, face to face. The whole time I kept asking this creature over and over "Who are you? Why are you here? What do you want?" Its only response was, "I came for the Keys." It turned out that his name was Roy. He was an Imp. I had never seen an Imp before that's why I thought he might be a Gremlin. He said that he was sent to get the keys that I had by a sorcerer named Sarin who lived in the seventh century. Sarin told Roy not to return without the keys, upon pain of death. My response was that I didn't know what he was talking about and even if I did I would never give any keys to him. I took the small Imp by his hand and transported back to the seventh century.

Sarin was a tall middle-eastern looking man with a

turban wound around his head. He was wearing a floor-length, ivory- colored silk robe. The front of his turban was adorned with a large red stone. It appeared to be a ruby the size of a small egg. I bluntly told Sarin that if any harm befell the Imp I would return and personally deal with him. Then I unceremoniously departed. It was after 4:00 o'clock in the morning when I got home. I barely had time to catch the 4:07 as it sailed by my house. I scrambled up the boarding net draped over its side. There was not a sole on board and there was but a single sail unfurled powering this pirate's sloop. It was a large billowing spinnaker.

In the hold I found a glowing glass orb perched on a pedestal. I assumed it was the magical heart of Black Beard's pirate ship. Using it, I summoned a full crew of dead pirates along with all of their needed provisions. The destination was ... Sarin the Sorcerer and in moments we were at his castle on the Adriatic. First I ordered a single cannon ball be sent through an open window. It was followed by stunned silence then I had two sixteen pounders sent through the portico and once again there was no response. Next I ordered a sixteen cannon broadside and it breached the castle wall. The rampart was lowered down over the moat and Sarin the Sorcerer emerged slowly on his horse waving a white flag. Then, I sauntered up beside his horse and reversed time. He gazed in amazement as each of the catastrophic events he had just witnessed was reversed, then, the pirate ship itself disappeared backwards into the bank of fog. He invited me into his magically restored castle. There I opened the small time chest and stopped time. I searched for the 'Box' he wanted opened. It wasn't hard to find but it was larger than I had imagined. Upon closer inspection I recognized this box. There was no way I would ever give anyone the key to this box, for it was Pandora's box. I knew instantly that I would have to steal it and somehow dispose of it.

Beelzebub

I had no idea what I should do with Pandora's box. I was sure that Sarin would come looking for it and for me as well. An associate of mine suggested that I return Pandora's box to its original creator. Eventually I found out who created Pandora's box. It was made by slave Imps at the behest of Beelzebub. So I decided that was where I should return it. The only thing I knew about Beelzebub was that it was supposed to be some kind of a demon.

I transported to where Beelzebub was located. I emerged on the other side of an expanse of water, near a dark stone tower, in his subterranean world. The water there could have been a large moat or a lake or perhaps the slow moving river Styx. Since I had never seen Beelzebub before, I didn't know what to expect. I don't know if it had a gender. I assumed it could be a male, because it was so huge, so muscular and had a very unpleasant disposition.

Beelzebub was reclining on a hewn stone platform with a sloping incline supporting his back. He had to weigh more than two thousand pounds. His long forearms were oddly shaped and were covered with dark, shiny, armored material. He was holding a huge cup filled with what looked like human blood in the hand portion of the arm appendage on his left side. His long, bifid, snake-like tongue shot out of his mouth, lapped up a load of blood and slid quickly back into his small ugly head. His dimly lit chasm, embedded deep within a labyrinth, was damp and smelled of dead roaches, though none were visible. His segmented compound eyes stared unblinking at me as I approached toting Pandora's box. He twisted his segmented, short neck to one side and asked of his guards, what was this irreverent thing approaching, unannounced and uninvited.

I put Pandora's box down on the floor directly in front of Beelzebub. I'm sure that he recognized it immediately as the prize jewel of his past creations. I told him that I was returning it and then I stood up straight staring deep into his bug eyes instead of bowing low like all of the other sycophants surrounding him. He shifted his heavy body only slightly as his long prehensile bifid tongue shot out to strangle my impudence.

I opened the tiny time box with the decoupage dome lid which I always carry hidden beneath my shirt. Time instantly stopped. Beelzebub's tongue froze inches from my face. I swiftly lopped off the last two feet of it with my short sword, then stuffed it into the leather pouch and tied it securely to my belt. As I departed this subterranean fortress I closed the time box. A loud roar followed me into the time tunnel then echoed quickly into a faded memory.

From there I went directly to Sarin's castle where I surreptitiously dropped the stone weighted pouch into the moat there where I was sure that Beelzebub would find it. Sarin would have a huge challenge in explaining to Beelzebub the loss of Pandora's box and the missing tongue being found in the moat of his own castle. This perhaps would give Sarin and Beelzebub pause before attempting to pursue me into the future where I now reside. I am sure that neither of them could possibly imagine how I had single-handedly stolen Pandora's box and chopped off Beelzebub's tongue and escaped from their armies of demons, Imps and Goblins.

Blue Goop

One of the girls I work with asked me to see if someone had cast a spell or put a curse on her because so many things had been going badly for her lately. I doubted that to be true but I agreed to check it out anyway the next time I was out and about. It was after midnight when I finished up with other chores and went out and about. I reminded her before hand that her dogs would probably go berserk when I arrived and that there was no way to know in advance how she would perceive my presence. The next day at work, she told me that her dogs had indeed gone crazy and woke her about 12:30 in the morning. She heard what sounded like a loud motorcycle hovering right over her roof, like a helicopter would do but there was nothing there, just the loud sound. I explained to her that I indeed was hovering above her and her brain was merely trying to interpret something that had no physicality, in a manner that seemed to create a logical coherent explanation, thus the sound of a loud motorcycle engine hovering above her like a helicopter might do. It sounds weird but the brain does funny things when it encounters something from another dimension or another reality.

What I saw, to my surprise, was some kind of blue goopy stuff in a few splotchy places on the backs of her hands and also completely covering her entire back. That of course was not normal, so I assumed that it had to be some sort of jinx or spell, or even worse... maybe a curse. I had no idea what the blue goopy stuff was or where it came from or for that matter what I should do with it. I proceeded to scrape the blue stuff off of the backs of her hands and then off of her back. Then, I placed it into two separate one-gallon pickle jars. It filled one completely and half of the second jar. I screwed the lids down tightly then, stored the stuff securely, until I could decide what to do with it.

About every three or four seconds, another splat of the blue goop would come shooting out of somewhere and it started to re-cover her back. I didn't know where it was coming from or what it was but I knew that I needed to put some kind of protective shell around her to keep the stuff from re-accumulating. So, I wound a long brown, woody, rope-like material which I found near by, around and around her, until she was completely covered from head to toe with this material, forming a cocoon like structure that prevented this blue goop from hitting her. I left it at that for the time being. It would have to wait until I could figure out what to do next. The goopy material accumulated on the woody cocoon that was protecting her but she was safe inside for the time being. The next day I asked her if she felt more secure and she said that she did.

I asked the Facilitator if he had any ideas about what this blue goop was or where it had come from. He said that he had no idea what it was or where it had come from. Then, I asked the Facilitator who I should ask to accompany me when I went back to re-investigate the situation and try to determine where it was coming from and what the stuff was, as well as who was behind the whole thing. The Facilitator suggested that I go alone at first and try to determine if this process originated in our dimension or from another dimension, as well as who or what was creating the disturbance, before deciding who or what resources would be appropriate to recruit for this endeavor. The Facilitator felt strongly that if I returned alone to re-evaluate the situation, it would create less of a disturbance and I would be better able to determine what exactly we were dealing with.

Untold Story

The next night, I returned looking for the source of the blue goop. It seemed to be materializing out of thin air about a hundred feet or so away, and coming towards me from due south. I have never encountered anything quite like that before. It materialized as a whirling spherical mass of small sparkling objects less than two centimeters in diameter. I approached it cautiously, not knowing if it were some kind of creature and not knowing what dimension or reality it came from. This cloud would form itself into a spherical shape almost thirty inches in diameter. It would begin to whirl as it materialized. Then, it would continue to whorl rapidly for about three or four seconds, before it would shoot off at very high speed and go splat onto the cocoon-like structure I had assembled around the girl from the office the night before, to protect her.

I needed to get a better look at this thing, so I opened the little magic box with the domed lid and time stopped. The whirling objects froze in the midst of forming into a sphere. From the left side was attached a dark sky blue ribbon made of something. This ribbon of material separated into all of these many small pieces. Out of the opposite side of the spherical mass of particles, was emitted a very thin, pale, wisp of a ribbon, that left the sphere along the same path of trajectory as the larger dark blue ribbon had entered the sphere. I tried to establish telepathic communication with the particles. The only information I was able to extract from the glittering particles was "Untold Story."

Whatever this thing ultimately turned out to be, I needed to stop it now. I took out my infinitely expandable magical leather pouch and stuffed the entire spherical mass of particles inside, before cinching it securely with its leather binding strings. When I closed the domed lid of the magic box, time began again but nothing happened inside of the pouch. Animation was suspended inside of the pouch. Time must cease to exist inside of this magic pouch.

Next, I needed to get rid of this 'Untold Story', whatever that was. I decided to take it into Dream Time and see if Aru, the 'Keeper of Dream Time' could help me get rid of this 'Untold Story'. I took the story and transported directly to Dream Time. Aru greeted me upon my arrival there. He asked me what I had in the bag and what I planned to do with it. When I told him that it apparently was an 'Untold Story,' Aru told me that since no one knew what the story was, there was no way it could be released safely in Dream Time. I needed to take it back with me and deal with it there where I got it.

From there, I returned to the cocoon covered with blue goop. First I removed the bulk of the goop that had accumulated since the night before and put it into a fifty-five gallon steel drum. This blue stuff almost filled the drum completely. Then, I split the cocoon open vertically with my magic sword, 'The Sword of Truth'. I wanted to make sure that the girl from the office was still O.K. Out of the opening stepped this tall thin female with wings. She was a beautiful woman dressed in a long ivory colored, floor-length, long sleeve gown, made of natural silk. I asked her who she was. She told me that she was the 'Moth of Time'.

In my conversation with the 'Moth of Time', she told me that she had been attracted (summoned) to assist the girl that works with me at the office, by the fervent unending prayers of the girl's mother, when she was almost four years old, because her mother was so concerned that her daughter was not doing well and might not survive. The mother apparently prayed to Christ and to Mary every night. In so doing, she actually summoned through her devotion and her determination, the 'Moth of Time', whose name turned out to be Christina Marie Barthon. When I asked if she were an angel, she emphatically replied, "I am not an angel. I am the Moth of Time. I transport people into the future or into the past and then return them safely back to their own time!"

I asked the beautiful Moth, if the girl from my office would be O.K. now. The Moth of Time thanked me for liberating her. When I split open the protective cocoon with my 'Sword of Truth,' it separated her spirit from the girl's spirit. She said that the girl from the office would be normal from now on but she would no longer be able to travel through time. That ability was only made possible by the connection that had been between her and the Moth of Time that now no longer existed. I asked if they would be joined together again at some future time. The 'Moth of Time' said that they would once again be joined into one, at the time of the girl's death but until then, the Moth would be free to travel the tunnels of time unimpeded once again and the girl would now be a normal person and no longer be capable of the magic of time travel and her obsessive compulsive behavior was gone permanently. Later that night I went to visit the daughter of the girl that works at my office, with the Moth of Time, to take her safely into the future so that she would see for herself that her future was bright. She would meet a boy while finishing college that she would marry. His name is Carlos Rudolfo Lopez. He goes by the name of Rudy. He is two or three months younger than her daughter. They will plan to marry on March 17th of 2017 because Rudy's favorite saint is St. Patrick but for some reason the wedding will be delayed until March 27, 2017. They will have 2 children together, a girl and a boy. Rudy will work in his family's business.

    The next day, when I went out to the back yard, there were hundreds and hundreds, if not thousands of small moths whirling around at extremely high speed in a spherical pattern. I have never seen anything like that, ever before, anywhere. I pointed them out to my wife. She didn't know what to make of them either. When I asked the girl at the office if she had seen anything like the moths at her house. She was shocked that I asked and said, "Yes, the little moths were all over the place flying around in a spherical pattern, going like crazy." She also had never seen anything like that before. I asked her to ask her daughter who was visiting in

California for five days if she had seen any moths. The daughter said that the little moths were everywhere and had even been following her around for two days.

The next night I summoned the 'Moth of Time' and asked her if she knew anything about these little moths. She said that the moths would follow her everywhere that she interacted with humans and transported them through time.

The next day I went out to the back yard to check on the moths. There was not a single moth in the whole yard. I asked the girl that works at the office about the moths. She told me that all of the moths had disappeared. Not a single moth was left at her house, which happens to be more than twenty miles from my house, in the middle of the desert.

Apparently, I assumed that the 'Untold Story' was, that the mother of the girl that works at the office prayed so fervently for the health and well being of her young daughter to improve that she had entangled her daughter and the 'Moth of Time. I inadvertently separated them with my 'Sword of Truth' while trying to remove what was supposed to be a curse. But eventually I will find out, that the Untold Story is about something else entirely.

Irwin

Yesterday afternoon my son called me when he was on his way home from his office. He said that something was at his house but he didn't know what it was or where it was located. He asked me to come over and get rid of it. I told him it would probably be after midnight before I would be able to get there. It was actually 12:06 in the morning when I woke up. I wasn't sure whom I wanted to take with me to help complete this project. In the end I decided to take Destiny, the magic white horse, Lucky, the six-year old little boy, Sabatini the Traveler's Buddha, the huge magic lion I refer to as the Facilitator and Christina Marie Barthon, the Moth of Time. We all transported over together from my back yard into my son's back yard and arrived near the large swimming pool.

To each of them, I assigned a different entranceway to cover. To the lion, I gave responsibility for two adjacent sets of French doors for two adjacent bedrooms. While they watched all of the doors, I checked out the three-car garage and the room above it, as well as the basement and then the attic. I found nothing in those places. So next I went through the back door and had Destiny, the magic white horse, follow me into the house. I checked out the entire place room by room, while everyone converged behind me into the living room. It was there where I finally located this strange character standing up on the heavy open beams that were supporting the roof.

This creature appeared differently to me depending on which method I used to observe it. With my normal vision, it was invisible. With the rose-colored spectacles, it appeared as pale vertical striations of translucent colors. With the reflection from the Sword of Truth, it was transformed into an unstable field of shifting energy. But, with the use of the magic pince-nez double lensed glasses, it became a two dimensional red devil, made of woven shiny polyester fabric, with a boyish face, tiny horns and a long thin tail that ended in a distinct point. I talked it into coming down out of the rafters and we sat down at the large round wooden table in the center of the living room to talk. The red devil took out a stack of ¼ inch thick rune-like objects, approximately 3 & ½ inches by 1 & ½ inches, with straight sides and rounded ends. He began placing them on top of the table like one would do with a bunch of fortune telling cards. When he was finished there were twenty-five of these rune-like things lined up next to each other, in a row.

This character referred to himself as Irwin. I use the term "He" because it looked a little like a 'He.' It had somehow come through the time tunnel and was now unable to return to the 5th dimension from whence it came. The first of the challenges for me was to establish communications with this strange being. The second and even more troubling problem for me was the time factor. In the 5th dimension, time is fragmented, not sequential or coherent in nature, like time is for us here in our dimension. This creature was also fragmented. It consisted of 25 separate parts, each existing in a separate piece or slice of time. That is what Irwin was trying to show me with the 25 objects it laid out on the table. Each rune represented a separate and distinct component of this creature.

I have been working in the fourth dimension and with the fourth attention recently. That is how this creature Irwin ended up at my son's house. I also just finished up a project with the Moth of Time. During that project I acquired a large quantity of 'blue goop' that I didn't know what to do with. This blue sticky goop is comprised of pure time, the past, the present and the future all combined together.

The solution I came up with consisted of first, stopping time by opening the lid of the magic domed box, second, putting a ring of this goop around all 25 of the rune pieces on the table, then scooping up the whole lot, including the creature itself and putting it into a cardboard box. I closed the box by folding the four corners of the tops under each other and pushed it into the containment sack where time doesn't exist. I closed the magic box, re-starting time, before transporting to the fourth dimension with it. Once in the fourth dimension, I asked two contacts I know there, Daniel and Zeke, to take me to the edge of the fourth dimension where I located a time vortex created by the eddy currents from the close proximity of the two different dimensions with their two different time systems. I moved to the very edge of the vortex, opened the containment sack, tumbled out the cardboard box, picked it up and tossed it into the center of the vortex. That action returned the creature back into its own dimension and time. I will have to check on Irwin's status later to see if the blue goop created any lasting, detrimental time-distortion problems for him.

Resolving the situation and successfully removing this visitor took me over three hours. There is an open time portal into my son's living room that has been there for several weeks. It is a by-product of a recent project I have been working on. I told my son that it was there and that I would close it as soon as I figured out how to do so but in the mean time, he should let me know if any more strange things showed up at his house.

I returned to my son's house and gathered up the entire expeditionary party and returned everyone safely back home. Two days later, my son finally called and told me that everything was just fine. Whatever was there at his house was gone now and his house felt normal once again.

The Taskmaster

On Friday the 22nd of December Stephen died from a drug overdose. He was forty-three years old. That does not bode well for him. We were in Orange County visiting for the Christmas holidays. I went looking for Stephen early on the morning of the twenty-fourth of December. I found him sitting on the curb in front of his parent's house. He was still completely wasted so I took him into their house and dumped him on a bed and left him there to sober up. He of course had no idea that he was dead.

Late that evening, on Christmas Eve, my wife and I were sitting on the sofa in front of the fireplace in the living room. My wife was watching the fire and I was reading a book to my Granddaughter. My wife said to me that she just saw someone walk past her into the family room. Later she elaborated on what she had seen. She said that she saw a woman walk by her out of the corner of her eye. The woman was wearing a black, floor-length, hooded robe that covered her face.

Later after everyone had retired for the evening, I went looking for this hooded woman. It didn't take me too long to find her. I asked her if she were death. She said that she wasn't death but an assistant who had been sent to gather up Stephen and take him to the 'Taskmaster' to be given appropriate punishment. That didn't sound too encouraging to me. I asked to see her face. She was a skeleton. I asked her why she was here bothering me. She said that when she went looking for Stephen, he was nowhere to be found, so she followed my trail from his parent's house to where I was staying there in California.

I told her that I needed to talk with her supervisor. Maybe we could cut a deal with respect to Stephen's proscribed punishment. Her supervisor turned out to be an assistant taskmaster and he had no authority to make any deals whatsoever. So, from there we went to the see the Taskmaster. He was dressed all in black and was sitting at a small desk engrossed in his paper work. I asked the Taskmaster about cutting some deal on Stephen's behalf. He insisted that he had to follow protocol and could not deviate from the proscribed punishment. Only the 'Assignment Angel' could alter that punishment. I said, "Well, let's go then to see the Assignment Angel." All three of them went with me.

I have had several encounters with the Assignment Angel. She is never happy to see me. She told me that Stephen was not supposed to die for twenty-five years so something would have to be done with him until then. His case was not being assessed strictly as a suicide but he had to be punished for his contribution to his own early demise. She said I needed to have an acceptable alternative proposal otherwise; the Taskmaster would punish him as customary. We all left the assignment Angel together. I went back to California to come up with some acceptable plan.

What I came up with was to have Stephen spend the next twenty-five years in the cave with the Buddha of the Mountain. I visited the Buddha first to make sure it was acceptable to him before I asked Death's Assistant to share my plan with the Assignment Angel and get her approval. When she returned with the authorization from the Assignment Angel's approval parts of her face were covered in flesh.

The next challenge for me was to locate Stephen. I finally found him wandering the streets of the red light district in Bangkok, Thailand. I grabbed him by the scruff of his neck and we transported together into the Buddha's cave, where I informed him that he was dead and that he had to stay there meditating for twenty-five years. After that, the Assignment Angel would assign him to his next life. The alternative was to be severely punished by the Taskmaster.

When Death's assistant and I went together to tell the Assignment Angel that Stephen was now with the Buddha, the Assignment Angel fleshed out the face of death's assistant and gave her the scroll for her next life. She vanished as she accepted the scroll. The Assignment Angel gave me a frown and then she also disappeared leaving me alone in what always reminds me of the Bonneville Salt Flats.

Damian

The Source insisted that I return again and again to Hades each time with specific additional tasks for me to accomplish. This has been on going now for a couple of weeks. I eventually was able to locate the three Furies. They were located on a tiny island situated in the middle of a very wide part of the river Styx. The Furies are the three goddesses of vengeance. Tisiphone is the avenger of murder, Megaera is for jealousy and Alecto is for constant anger. They are the daughters of Uranus and Gaea.

Hades was supposed to be filled with demons but I was unable to locate a single one. After much effort I finally acquired the ability to see these demons but that required the ability to process a different form of non-light vision. Purgatory was also supposed to be attached to Hades but again I was unable to visualize it until I mastered a third form of non-light sight.

I eventually located a woman frozen in Purgatory like in the movie Ground Hog's Day where everything was repeated over and over every day for her. It was a bizarre experience for me. She had been there since committing suicide in the year 1917 when she was informed that her fiancée was killed in the 1st World War. She jumped off of a bridge. Her name was Nancy and she was six months pregnant at the time of her death. It took me awhile but I managed to free her up and get her on the way to resolution. As she began to make progress she began moving upward in an expanding transparent tube of some sort. The Source wanted me to get someone out of Purgatory as my next assignment.

I took a short cut and figured out how to extricate Nancy since she had already done her time there and had momentum and was moving rapidly up and out of Purgatory on her own. Once I got her out of Purgatory I put her in a safe place temporarily. This did not sit well with the Source who wanted me to understand the process more completely that was required for extrication of one from Purgatory.

I discovered that each individual was inside a transparent tube. There were several tiny threads attached to them like spider webs. If I touched one of these threads demons quickly responded. I needed to figure out a way to work around this alarm system.

For my next rescue I chose a giant creature that was on the surface of Hades and not inside of a tube. He was big and ugly and had a thick steel collar around his neck that was anchored down by a heavy chain to a cement pier. I stopped time and put a bubble of time around both of us then I severed the chain and we floated up to the surface and out of Purgatory.

I asked who and what he was. He said that his name was Damian and he was a demon. He told me that everyone hated him for all the bad things he always did. I told him that I was his friend. I had set him free and he could travel with me on my many adventures but from now on he could only do good things. He agreed to those conditions and I removed the heavy steel collar from around his neck and took him to the same safe place where I had taken Nancy and introduced him to the inhabitants there as their protector.

The Night Bus, September 26th

I awoke this morning a few minutes before the Night Bus was due to pass by our house at 2:00 o'clock. I thought I should catch the bus and go somewhere but I wasn't sure exactly where that should be. The Night Bus rounded the corner at the end of our street at 1:59 a.m. Two houses before it arrived in front of our house, it stopped briefly for about 30 seconds. The Night Bus had never done that before. Then, the bus proceeded on to our house, where it stopped again to pick me up.

Brad, the bus driver, opened the doors to the bus to allow me to jump on. I climbed the steps into the bus. As

I was telling the bus driver I wanted to go to the twelfth attention, I looked towards the back of the bus. It was jammed full with thirty-seven children. All of the seats were completely full instead of being empty as usual.

As the bus began moving ahead, every child melted into a shiny puddle of different-colored, iridescent liquid. At the same time, the bus driver and I melted into separate puddles of colored liquid ourselves. When the bus stopped, everyone was instantly reconstituted into his or her former selves, all at the same time.

I asked Brad what had just happened. He told me that when he stopped momentarily two houses down from our house, the bus filled to capacity with sick and dying children because they somehow knew, even before I did, that I was going to the twelfth attention. There, they might have a chance to get their health restored. In fact, when they were reconstituted, they were all once again healthy and whole.

I stepped out of the Night Bus and into what looked like an empty classroom, devoid of all furnishings except for a large blackboard covering one wall, some chalk and an eraser.

When I questioned the "Source" about this place, he told me that this was the twelfth attention and this was the place from which all health and wellbeing emanated. He said that it was up to me to accumulate all of the various tools that I would need to be able restore the health and well-being to anyone who was in need of such assistance.

I assume that this refers to all other animals just as

well as people but that remains to be seen.

The Oreo Brigade

At 1:57 a.m. I went out to the front yard to catch a ride on the Night Bus. The old bus turned the corner at the end of our street a little before 2:00 o'clock. It wobbled from side to side as it slowly came down the street towards our driveway. I expected the bus to be crammed full of crazy kids jumping all over the place but when the bus driver opened the door and I climbed up the steps into the bus and looked around, the bus was completely empty. I told Brad, the bus driver, I needed to go to the twelfth attention, the source of all health and healing. As he put the bus in gear and the bus started moving, I drew my trusty 'Sword of Truth' and looked into its shiny surface to see what might actually be there in the bus. It was completely full of translucent people, all with round bald bulbous heads, staring at me through their gaunt bulging eyeballs. I asked Brad who they were. He told me they were all totally insane. He said they were all going to the twelfth attention because it was their last and only hope of becoming sane once again.

Brad stopped the bus and I jumped out through the open door and landed in a large classroom devoid of any furnishings, with a giant blackboard along one wall. This was the twelfth attention. All ninety insane souls from the night bus tumbled in after me. I had no idea what to do with all of these crazy people. I had no tools or strategies for dealing with this sort of affliction. They all stared endlessly at me with their unblinking eyes, as they crowded ever closer with their outstretched arms and grasping fingers. I needed to come up with some sort of plan and it had to be quickly.

They were all totally insane. They were all totally disconnected from physical reality. I grabbed a package of OREO cookies lying on the desk. My only thought was, "No one can resist an OREO cookie." As they reached out to grab me I placed an OREO in each grasping hand and whispered in each ear, "A taste of reality."

The delicious taste of an honest to goodness real OREO cookie melting in their mouth reconnected them to the real world and brought them back to their senses. One by one they disappeared from the twelfth attention and returned to the world of physical reality, no longer insane but completely cured by the unforgettable taste of a genuine OREO cookie.

Coyote's Howl

It was September 24th, the night of the Harvest Moon. It was after midnight. I was talking with the Source. As we walked along in the light from the full moon he said to me that he was giving me the 'Gift of Life'. I heard a coyote's mournful howl in the distance. I was very excited to receive the 'Gift of Life'. What a magnificent gift to share with others. He then told me that with the 'Gift of Life' came the 'Curse of Death'. I was very distraught because that was the last thing I wanted to have. I told the Source that I could never be trusted with the 'Curse of Death', for surely I would begin killing all of those I felt were justly deserving of such a fate. The Source elaborated, "There is no good without evil. There is no Yin without Yang." He said that I must decide for he would not again offer to bestow this 'Gift of Life' upon me. I didn't know what to do. What a magnificent gift... What a horrible curse.

The coyote howled three times. It was closer now. I went to visit the coyote and shape-shifted myself into a coyote and sat down in front of it in the moonlight. I shared my dilemma with the Wise and Wiley coyote. He said that I must accept the gift that was offered to me. When I complained about the curse that accompanied this gift. He said, "A dog without a bite is all bark and not a real dog at all." I returned and informed the Source that I would accept the "Gift of Life" The coyote howled three times. The Source then gave me the 'Curse of Death." The coyote howled six times and my Fate was sealed. I asked the Source if the gift of life could be bestowed upon another person from a distance. He said that the 'Gift of Life' could only be transferred by touch because life is a physical state but the 'Curse of Death' could be delivered by coming out from within the dreamscape like Freddy Kruger, for death is a non-physical state.

A couple of hours later, I heard the coyote howl mournfully in the distance. My wife began to shake and gasp for breath in her sleep. I was afraid she might be dying. I touched her. I shared the 'Gift of Life' with her and she returned to a peaceful state of sleep. In the distance, the coyote howled twice with seeming satisfaction.

In the morning, my wife shared a strange dream she had during the night. She said that she was at a gathering where two of her great uncles greeted her happily with hugs and adulation. She asked them if they knew who she was, for she had not seen them since she was a young girl. They said of course they knew who she was. There were several other people gathered there as well. All of them now long since dead and buried.

Tortuga

This morning I was awake at 3:40 a.m. I wondered if anything unusual might be coming down the street in front of my house at 3:45 a.m., so I went out to the sidewalk and waited to see if anything might pass by.

A large annular ring of smoke or fog, about eighteen inches high and several feet in width rolled by, followed closely by a second annular ring of smoke and then a third ring, moving down the street like waves on a lake from some large object having been dropped into the water. I had no idea what kind of contraption could possibly create that kind of effect. I waited anxiously, to see what would come.

To my surprise, there was this huge tortoise, which had to weigh three or four hundred pounds. It definitely was not a Galapagos Tortoise. The carapace was different. It looked more like a Giant African Tortoise. It was moving its legs in a very mechanical way to a cadence quite clock-like, tick...tock...tick...tock ...tick...tock. At first I thought it must be a machine, but upon closer investigation, it was surely not. It was definitely alive, stopping for no one.

I approached the tortoise and engaged it in conversation. I asked the tortoise who he was and he told me that he was the Time Tortoise. I asked about the three rings of smoke or fog or whatever it was. The tortoise said that the first ring was the future, the second ring was the present and the third ring, was the past.

As we continued down the road, his pace was unrelenting. I asked why he came at 3:45 in the morning. He said that he came at 3:45 a.m. because he weighed three hundred and forty-five pounds. We were moving rapidly from place to place. I noticed that the tortoise left a trail of sparkly dust, like smoke from an oil-burning car or a diesel truck going up a steep grade in the mountains. The dust trail strung out behind us as far back into the distance as I could see. I asked the tortoise what that dust trail was. He told me that it was time.

Before long, we were traipsing through Grand Central Station. Surprisingly there weren't that many travelers there. Maybe 3:45 a.m. is not at the height of domestic travel.

A small boy, accompanied by both of his parents, approached me. His hair had fallen out in great patches and he looked emaciated as though he were dying from cancer or some other terrible disease. He came up to me and tugged at my pant leg as we passed by. He said, "Please, mister, please give me a little more time."

I asked the Time Tortoise if that trail of sparkling dust could actually give someone more time. The tortoise said that it could. "How much more time," I asked. He said, "Maybe five minutes, maybe five months, maybe five years, it all depends." So, I immediately scooped up a bunch of the dust and sprinkled it over the little boy's head. His hair returned to normal and his gaunt features were transformed into that of a normal healthy child. He said, "Thanks, mister. Thanks for giving me more time."

I took out my ever-expansive magic bag that I always carry with me and followed the Time Tortoise, scooping up as much time dust as I could carry because you never know when you might encounter someone who is running out of time and needs just a little more time to finish their job.

Smyth's

Once you have been someplace, you should know where you have been. The easiest and fastest way to travel back to that place, where you have been before, is to go point to point by portal. My visit to the tropical island left me with questions in my mind, about Cecil, the talking baby goat and the disappearing child, Eric. So, I returned to the tropical island seeking answers to those questions.

The kid goat was on the sandy beach when I arrived but not the child. I asked the white baby goat about the appearing, disappearing child, Eric. The kid goat informed me that Eric was not the child's name. I patted the baby goat on the head and asked him to tell me more about the child.

I found myself instantly in the cafeteria or lunchroom of a school or some other commercial establishment. There were only a couple of other people in there, beside myself. A tall thin dark-haired young lady approached and asked if I needed any assistance. I told her that I was just looking around and would be leaving momentarily. She came very close to me, sniffed my face and hair then, she continued with her sniffing down my left arm all the way to the tips of my fingers. She gave me a smile of approval, as though she had just checked out a loaf of bread for freshness at the bakery. She turned and departed through a pair of half-glass security doors and disappeared down a long hallway. The glass window portions of the doors had steel chicken wire embedded between two thick layers of rippled glass. I walked down a short passageway that joined the cafeteria at ninety degrees to the left of the security doors. On the right side of this passageway, there was a small alcove with a wooden cupboard door at its end. The door was made of thick heavy oak. It was at eye level and maybe two feet high and two or three feet wide. There was a rusty iron handle on the left side of the door. I forced it open with a big jerk. On the other side there was an African soldier standing just to the left side of the door with his AK-47. He was guarding a pickup truck filled with gaunt, dusty, frightened, African prisoners. There were maybe nine or ten of them huddled in the bed of a pickup truck. They were all young and they were all headed for the slaughterhouse. This whole place was dedicated to wholesale cannibalism. Here at Smyth's you could get anything you were willing to pay for, prepared any way you like it.

I knew then that I had to get out of there and fast. I ran back down the passageway, across the expansive cafeteria floor and out the sliding glass doors onto the open air dining area and jumped over the railing onto the hillside far below. That same young lady, who had sniffed me out, followed me onto the elevated porch and was yelling at me from the railing above, waving a large meat cleaver in her hand.

I ran down a dirt road that I thought would eventually lead to somewhere. The road finally ended in Granite Mountains in the middle of No Man's Land. There was a gigantic Tyrannosaurus Rex at least a hundred feet tall, looking for prey. It was apparently made of the same black and gray granite that the mountain itself was made from. When it stopped moving, it would disappear into the background of the mountains themselves. It obviously noticed me when I clambered under a big rock perched precariously on the side of the mountain. When it came looking for me, I was able to dislodge the boulder I was hiding under and it crashed down onto the giant dinosaur, distracting it while I escaped down a ravine. The ravine ran next to a hidden valley. There was a small opening in the wall of the ravine, which I was able to crawl through after breaking a couple of roots that were obstructing my passage.

In the hidden valley, there were four children, three young girls and a boy. The boy said that he was fifteen, though he looked to be younger. Two of the girls said they were eleven, though they appeared to be nine and ten respectfully. The third girl was probably five or six years old, but she said that she was nine.

From there I was once again, instantly on the island with the talking baby goat. I realized at that moment, the goat was not talking to me, but it was communicating telepathically, providing me with his perspective on the life of a young goat. The children I saw represented the life situation for goats, where some goats are eaten as kids, others are saved for breeding purposes. Most of the male goats are slaughtered. A few are used for breeding but not until they are the human equivalent of fifteen years of age. Those female goats to be used for future breeding were picked out of the herd, at the human equivalent age of nine years but not bred until the human equivalent age of eleven years. There were no old people, ergo, no old goats, of either gender, meaning that they were all slaughtered and eaten by humans or wild animals.

That would explain why the young boy wanted to be fifteen and the nine and ten year old females wanted to be eleven, and the five or six year old wanted to be nine. Those were the ages that mattered most in the scheme of things, from a goat's perspective.

The baby white goat was telling me this story telepathically by comparing their lot as young goats, to what would be children for humans. The child that was there and then gone and there again and then half gone, being halved along the vertical axis, represented what happens to baby goats. They arrive whole in the meat market but are sold as half or as whole dressed animals for human consumption. They appear and then they disappear. Like a puppy in the window of a pet store, first they are there and then they are gone. To be replaced by yet another young innocent animal.

I asked the baby white goat about the Tyrannosaurus I saw, made of granite. He said the granite mountain itself consumes many baby goats from the cold and the heat, the wind and the drought, and the dangers from the rocky cliffs, not to mention the many predators that lurk there amongst the granite boulders, especially we humans.

Such is the fate of goats. They eat...they breed...they die...they are eaten.

Symbolically, our lot as humans may not be that

much different than that of a baby goat, a little white kid.

Maurice

Last night at 3:15 a.m. my wife said that there was something in the bedroom. I checked the situation out. Things seem to always come to her side of the bed, in part because the bedroom door is on her side of the room. I could see a young girl standing next to my wife's side of the bed and some big something filling the doorway. It takes a little while for me to be able to focus on these visitors to see them well enough to give an accurate description of them and to determine why they are there.

The girl was thin with fairly light complexion but not pale white. She was about nine years old. She had two unbraided pigtails sticking straight out of the side of her head. Her hair was straight and dark brown. She had on black Mary Jane shoes with white socks folded down at the top one turn. Her dress was plaid, short with a full skirt and bib type front with wide straps going over her shoulders and crossing in the back before attaching to a waistband. Her blouse was white with short puffy sleeves. Both arms were extended out with a small plate held by both hands. On top of the plate was a folded piece of white paper. It was folded halfway like a napkin or part of a paper airplane with one bent wing and its nose sticking straight up.

I asked several questions of her but she remained silent and stationary, with her arms extended towards my wife. I asked who she was and why she was there and what she wanted. I asked her several times to come to my side of the bed but there was no response. Eventually I reached over and opened the folded paper. On it was a printed message for my wife, "I Love You." Upon closer observation, the girl looked familiar. I asked her if she were Aida. She shook her head up and down. "Did you come to tell your Auntie Virginia that you loved her?" She again shook her head slowly up and down, and then said that her Auntie Virginia had had a very bad day and needed to know that she was loved.

Then I turned my attention to the large creature filling the doorway. I asked it to come over to my side of the bed. It was actually quite large, at least seven feet tall, with a huge head and equally large mouth with sharp-pointed, yellow teeth. It was very plump and covered with long shaggy dark brown hair. Its eyes were also very large. Its hands were fat and totally covered with hair.

When I asked it to come to my side of the bed, it didn't hesitate but waddled right over to my side. I said to it, "You look like the Wild Thing. You aren't the Wild Thing are you?"

He told me that he was the 'Wild Thing'. I told him I didn't know that there actually was a Wild Thing. When I asked him what he was doing there with Aida, he said that he followed her from where she lived with her parents in their house near the forest where he lived outside of Boston because she had a vivid imagination.

I asked the Wild Thing if he would like to stay in Never Land with the bears and the dogs, the unicorns, the three lions and the baby dragon. He said for sure he would like that. I told him to step over the bridge but not on it because I didn't want him to break it and then I introduced him to all of the creatures and left him there.

"If I'm not mistaken, didn't Maurice Sendak, the creator of the 'Wild Thing' live near Boston before he passed on?"

The Return of the Three Crows

Today is the fifteenth, the day of the full moon. Crows come bearing a gift every full moon. I just never know when they will arrive. So, I check in the morning and in the evening.

This morning, three crows were outside my bedroom window walking around, looking in and appearing anxious. I went outside to check on them but they seemed to be totally disorganized, so I left and took care of some other business. A couple of hours later I returned to find the same three crows milling around. When I went outside to see them, they all three lined up in a row like chorus dancers, or Vaudeville performers and began singing:

"Happy birthday to you... happy birthday to you... happy birthday Michael..." They paused at a loss for what came next, looked around at each other then began singing again. "Happy birthday, Michael, Michael... Happy birthday to you." There was another short pause, before the larger crow piped in with his baritone crow voice, "And many more... Michaels..." Then they all looked back and forth at each other, laughed loudly together, slapping each other on the back with their wing feathers, then they all flew away into the night sky. This seemed totally nuts to me, but I looked around for any gifts they might have left behind. There, behind where the crows had just performed, was a very large gray egg with brownish red spots. The egg was larger than an ostrich's egg but more oblong and it was less perfectly shaped. I went over and picked it up and took it inside the house. The egg was very heavy, much heaver than even lead. It must have weighed at least 100 pounds even though it wasn't more that eleven or twelve inches in length.

    I carried the large egg inside and put it on the floor in my bedroom, next to the bed. A couple of hours later, when I looked at the egg, it had almost doubled in size. I put on the rose-colored glasses and through them, the egg appeared to be perfectly shaped and perfectly white with a halo of shimmering yellow light around it. When viewed as a reflection from the Sword of Truth, I could see through the shell of the egg, and into its inner contents. There appeared to be a large hooked beak, two large open eyes, and a body that didn't look at all like a bird. There was a humming sound coming from the egg. When I touched the egg, it was vibrating.

I kept my hand on the egg for a couple of minutes and the sound and the vibrations slowly dissipated. The egg became quiescent.

Later in the morning, when I got up to get ready to go to the office, the egg had quadrupled in size, but its weight had remained unchanged. The contents looked more ominous, yet more familiar. To me it looked like a growing Griffin.

Later that night, when I was ready to go to sleep, I checked on the egg once again. It was much, much larger than it was in the morning, but still weighed the same. When I inspected its contents using the reflection from the sword, the egg immediately began to vibrate and hum loudly. By placing my hand on the egg it began to quiet down and the vibrations dissipated. This reminded me, a little, of a purring cat. I assumed that by touching the egg, some level of communication was being established.

I needed to think through this situation, before deciding what I should do with this ever-enlarging egg before it was too big to move through the doorway or it hatched.

Where Wild Things Sleep

After much consideration, I concluded that the best place for a growing egg like this to be located was in Never Land. As far as I know, a griffin is a mythical and probably a magically creature, so what better place could there be.

I crossed over the bridge that leads to Never Land, located the Wild Thing, and had him come back to help move the growing egg from my bedroom to the open area beneath the large tree in the middle of the meadow where the Wild Thing slept. The Wild Thing walked through the stream holding his end of the egg, while I walked back over the bridge into Never Land, carrying the other end of the egg as we returned.

Once we had the egg situated, I gathered all of the animals around the egg and told them that they needed to have personal contact with the egg, so that the new arrival would be comfortable around them and not try to eat them for dinner after it hatched. They were all excited about a new arrival, especially a baby Griffin if that turned out to be the case.

I went back a few hours later to check on the status of the egg only to find all of the animals piled around the growing egg like a pile of stuffed animals in a child's toy box. I'm concerned about what the possibilities are when the egg finally hatches. I will check periodically and try to anticipate hatching day. With the rapid rate of growth of the egg, it can't be too many days before we find out who our new guest is.

The next night, I returned to check on the status of the growing egg four times. Each time the egg was larger and each time I made progress. At first I could only see the contents of the egg from the sword's reflections but later I was able to see directly into the egg by using some unknown new capacity. At first there was this snapping sound from inside the griffin egg as it rapidly bit down with its curved beak. Later it stopped doing this when I touched the egg. At first the egg vibrated and hummed loudly but later this also stopped when I touched the egg. At first, this angry eye would stare intently out at me but later the eye would open initially but then close as the griffin went back to sleep. As I visited with the egg more times, there was some sort of circular connecting made directly between my brain and the brain of the griffin. Perhaps this was from imprinting like a bird, or bonding of some kind.

Later still, just before dawn, I returned and advised all of the humans who reside there in Never Land that they must make personal contact with the egg before it hatches for their own safety. I also reminded the leprechauns that they too had to establish personal contact with the griffin egg before it hatched for their own safety.

It was quite a sight to see all of these magical creatures attending to the griffin egg, the lions, the bears, the baby dragon, the unicorns, the dogs, the people, the leprechauns, and especially the Wild Thing.

From there, I went to Ireland to seek advice from the Wizard in the Glen. When I told him about the Griffin egg, he had an attack. He told me that Griffins are the most vicious creatures of all. I asked if he had ever even seen a griffin. He said no. I visited the wizard in search of truth regarding griffins, not seeking personal bias grounded in myth and conjecture.

Emory

We go back several years. I first met Emory after he unsuccessfully attempted to terminate me. He sent a man on horseback with a golden dagger to do the job. I believe the rider was an apprentice of his who unfortunately met up with his own untimely termination. A few days before that attempt on my life, a sorcerer in the hire of the Queen of England attempted to do the same. That attempt stripped the queen's personal sorcerer of all of his powers, though he still lives but in impotence, the ultimate disgrace for any sorcerer.

The last attempt on my life by Emory left him dying from the reversal of his own spells. It took great skill and immense power on my part to rectify that misadventure of his. He finally decided to give up with his quest to get rid of me. I visited him several times, nursing him back from the brink of death. He was born in 1602. I first met him in 1655, when he was 53 years old. He was baffled when I told him I had no friends or for that matter no enemies either, this after he had attempted to kill me several times. Your friends are not going to keep you out of trouble and your enemies are not going to get you into trouble, unless you allow yourself to be taken into harm's way. The last time I visited Emory, he was alive and well in 1657. I went in search of information about Griffins but he offered no help. He had never even seen a griffin.

Since I was given a Griffin Egg for my birthday, I have

been trying to figure out what to do with the Griffin when it hatches. Everyone I asked about griffins told me they were nothing but bad news. That may or may not be the case but I didn't want to place all of the residents of Never Land in harms way based on my own personal speculation. The prospect of moving the expanding Griffin egg became less and less plausible. After giving much thought to the situation and looming potential disaster that could ensue, I decided not to move the egg at all but to transport it into a different time. I asked the Wild Thing to assist me in this endeavor. Then, I left the Wild Thing in charge of looking after the well being of the egg while I was away in the future. I told him I would check on them both a couple of times each day while we were waiting for the big hatchling.

This morning at 12:07 a.m., I returned to check on the hatching process. The Wild Thing was asleep at the switch with his head resting on one end of the egg. I went to the other end of the egg and leaned against it waiting for the egg to begin to hatch. At 12:22 a.m., on the 22nd of January, my birthday, the Griffin began to break out of his egg. He ate his way out of the shell that was pliable like leather instead of brittle like a chicken egg. After he had freed his entire head, he lay his head down on my lap and rested. That strong loop- like mental connection between us was re-established and I was again able to communicate telepathically with the Griffin. I told the Griffin that his name was Griffin and that he should consider anyone who knew his name as a friend unless they tried to harm him.

He asked if I were his mother. I told him, "No, I am not your mother," but I said that The Wild Thing and I were his brothers and that we were part of his family, as was everyone else that he might encounter sometime in a future Never Land. I had taken the Griffin Egg back in time to before there were any humans so that he could be free to grow up and become all that a Griffin is supposed to be. I left the Wild Thing there as his companion, his brother, and his family. The Griffin shook his feathers dry and flew away alone into the night sky in search of himself. When the Wild Thing woke up, I asked him to wait there for Griffin to return. I told him the Griffin's name is Griffin, so always address him as such and everything will be just fine. I told the Wild Thing I would visit them as often as I could to check on the progress that Griffin was making.

From there I went to visit with Emory. He was surprised that I managed to move the Griffin that far into the past. He said it was an elegant solution to a very complex situation. He told me that he was proud that he knew me and glad that he was unsuccessful in his attempts to get rid of me, even if I had no friends.

Each night after that, I returned to the Griffin's new place in time. The first night I returned, the Wild Thing was waiting under the large tree by himself. He said that the Griffin had not returned, so I went looking for the Griffin. I found him in a large cave. I coaxed the Griffin out of the cave into the open and spent some time there with him. I left him there in front of his cave after he went to sleep. The next night when I returned,

I went into the Griffin's cave where he was sleeping. He wasn't growing any larger but he was filling in his frame and becoming more muscular and more mature. I spent a few hours there with him until he finally fell asleep with his nose on my lap. The next time I returned to the Griffin's cave he wasn't there.

Eventually, I found him sleeping under the tree with the Wild Thing. The Wild Thing was sleeping with his head on the Griffin's back end. I didn't disturb them but it was reassuring to find them back together. Last night when I went back to where they were in time, the Griffin was asleep with his head on the Wild Thing's lap. That was a really good sign that they had each other. They were family. Tonight I will return again to make sure things are progressing in a positive way.

I received the Griffin egg on the night of the full moon, the fifteenth of January, seven days before my birthday. The egg continued to grow in size for seven days and hatched on the twenty-second of January that was my birthday. The Griffin continued to grow after it hatched for seven days, then it just filled in its frame.

When I visited Emory after that, he asked how long Griffins lived. I told him that I had no idea. He said that if Griffins live forever, I should be prepared for Griffin to arrive on my doorstep, sooner or later.

I have thought about bringing Wild Thing and Griffin back from the past into our time but I can't do that until I know more about what Griffins are capable of doing.

The Hounds of Baskerville

Yesterday morning at a little after 4:30 a.m., my wife rolled over and said to me, "There's something here." That is always a request, not a statement. She always wants to know what the story is, as well as what is actually there.

There was nothing beside the bed but stretched across the open door to our bedroom was what appeared to be this large, gray, animal skin. It looked like a really big wolf skin. The snout was attached at the top of the lintel, in the center. The front paws stretched out horizontally and were attached over the sides of the doorjamb, while the two back legs were attached at the bottom corners. On the other side of the doorway, in the hall, were a bunch of big black dogs with brown muzzles that were barking and jumping around, trying to get past the outstretched gray wolf skin.

I never panic. I always follow a protocol. "Who are you? What do you want? Why are you here? What are those dogs doing jumping around in the hallway?" I was somewhat surprised that answers came quite quickly ...telepathically. From what I thought was an animal skin came the emphatic answer that she was the Gray Wolf of the North and she was keeping the Hounds of Baskerville at bay.

I got out of bed and went to the doorway, stuck my head around the big gray wolf and yelled at the hound dogs, "Get lost." In great surprise, they all froze with wide eyes and mouths falling open, turned quickly on their heels and dashed down the hall and out through the walls of the house. There appeared to be three or four of them but in the darkened hallway there may have been even more.

I invited the Gray Wolf of the North to come over to my side of the bed. She released her jaws clamped to the doorjamb, dropped to the floor and moved close to me beside the bed and sat down on her haunches. She was huge, far larger than any wolf I had ever seen. As I continued asking her one question after another, she provided me with strange and implausible answers.

She told me that her name was Tinian and she had come to the rescue because the Hounds of Baskerville were chasing my Cardigan Welsh Corgi. I asked the she wolf, how could that be, my dog was asleep in his bed there in our bedroom.

Her answer was that my dog was dreaming and the hounds began chasing him in his dream. The problem was that the walls of our house are riddled with holes and tunnels and portals and passageways from all of the many years of me traveling through them on my endless adventures in search of the 'Holy Grail'. That allowed the Hounds of Baskerville to fly right out of the dreamscape and right into our house. They would have gotten to my dog, the she wolf said, if it were not for her swift and decisive intervention.

I never pass up an opportunity to inquire, no matter how bizarre a situation might be, as to the acquisition of logical ancillary information. So I asked, if she were the Gray Wolf of the North, were there possibly... other cardinal wolves as well. She said, "Yes, there is the Wolf of the South, the Wolf of the West and also the Wolf of the East."

This sounded like an opportunity to me worthy of further investigation.

The Four Cardinal Wolves

Last night I summoned the four wolves one by one until all four of them were present together. First of all, I wanted to find out if there really were other wolves besides the Gray Wolf of the North and secondly, I wanted to have some idea what they might be capable of doing.

The first one of the wolves that I summoned was naturally the Gray Wolf of the North because we had already met the night before and she had demonstrated an impressive capacity to communicate clearly, which in and of itself could prove to be an invaluable asset.

The second wolf I summoned was logically the Wolf of the South. This wolf turned out to be a jet-black, male wolf, whose name was Buschard. Next I summoned the Wolf of the East. This wolf was a snow white, female wolf with the name Estrella. The last wolf, the Wolf of the West, was a red wolf whose name was Willis. That left me with four giant wolves, Tinian, Buschard, Estrella, & Willis.

When I put on the rose-colored glasses and looked at each of the wolves, their appearance changed. The white wolf became a single red rose. The black wolf turned into a white chrysanthemum. The red wolf was a red tulip and the gray wolf became a white jonquil. Next, I warned the four wolves that I would draw my trusty sword before I did, so they would have no reason to bolt at the sight of it. When I drew the sword and stared into its reflective surface, each of the wolves became a shade, a bizarre wispy creature associated with death and dying that comes straight from the underworld.

I remembered the golden disc that I wear on a gold chain around my neck at all times. It was a gift from Osiris, the Egyptian God of the Underworld. It has deep and permanent magic. It is a little more than six inches in diameter with a smooth lustrous surface, about one inch thick in the center and tapers off in a gentle curve towards its rounded edges. This disc emits the light of the full moon. It also provides me with clear passage through the underworld and protects me from any harm that originates in the underworld. It was indispensable during my many excursions into the realm of the dead.

As I cast the moonlight emitted from the glowing disc onto each shade, it disintegrated into a fine powder that fell to the ground forming a small conical pile. After the last shade disintegrated, I once again observed each wolf through the rose-colored glasses. Each individual flower was transformed into a large bouquet of flowers, a bouquet of red roses, one of white chrysanthemums, another of colorful red tulips and another of white jonquils.

I removed the glasses and once again there were four wolves staring at me in amazement. They began frolicking around, jumping, barking and playing together as only canidae can. They couldn't believe that they were free at last, free to be free, no longer tethered to the shades of the underworld. They were free to be what they were, agents of change. The four Cardinal Wolves, four agents of change, magical creatures capable of creating change in your life, in my life, in everyone's lives, ran into the meadow and it burst into a colorful display of endless spring flowers of every kind and color. Then each disappeared over the hill into their cardinal direction, leaving me alone in an endless field of flowers.

Admissions & Omissions

I admit, that frequently, I omit many details from these adventures, in an effort to simplify or to clarify a central theme and to confine the discussion to a single page when possible. Sometimes an omission becomes an important element in some unanticipated future encounter and of necessity must be re-visited for the sake of clarity and continuity.

OMISSION: After the four cardinal wolves split the scene, I was so impressed with the field of beautiful flowers that they left behind. I brought Griffin and Wild Thing to romp with me through their endless colors and fragrances. Wild Thing brought with him a banjo with a very long neck. It seemed so odd and out of character for him, but Wild Things, after all, are free to be wild.

Yesterday we all lost a dear friend, someone that most of us admired immensely, yet we never really met or understood Philip Seymour Hoffman. He was a giant among giants. As a character actor, there really were none better. I was concerned that he was vulnerable and in a difficult situation, so I went looking for him. I found him wondering around the streets of Greenwich Village. He was lost and wanted to go back to his apartment. I escorted him back to his apartment and left him fully clothed, completely stoned on his bed. I didn't know what else to do with him. I didn't want a narco stoner running amuck in Never Land. I needed to come up with an alternative solution. I believed he was at risk of becoming 'The Lost Ghost of Greenwich Village.'

I try to visit Griffin and Wild Thing every day, when I have the time. When I went there last night, they were together in Griffin's cave. Outside of the cave there were flowers everywhere, just like the flowers in the field where I last saw them. Inside the cave, Wild Thing was sleeping with that same banjo still in his left hand. "Eureka"! I put 'Two and Two' together. I went over to Griffin and pried his eyelid open and told him that I was leaving and would bring more of the family for a visit.

Last week we lost another giant whose long shadow

still colors our everyday music. Peter Seeger plays a banjo just like the one that Wild Thing had. I found Pete playing his banjo sitting on a tall stool in a crowded café singing, "Where have all the flowers gone…" I knew then that my 'eureka moment' had merit. I asked Pete if he really wanted to know where all the flowers had gone. He said yes and then we were gone. I left him in the flowers outside Griffin's cave, sitting on his stool playing his banjo and went for Philip. We returned to Griffin's Cave. I introduced everyone all around then I prepared to leave. As I departed I yelled back to Peter Seeger, "Play Pete play. Play Philip. Play him until he is sober."

The next night, I returned to see how they were doing. Peter was sitting on his stool in the flowers on one side of the fire and Griffin, Wild Thing and Philip were lined up on the other side listening to Peter play his banjo and sing, "Two plus Two are four…Two plus Two are four…" two giants from the entertainment world and two giants from the fantasy world. A new family of odd couples was created: a couple of entertainers and a couple of magical creatures, a great solution to a perplexing problem for me.

Seeger & Seymour

Two days ago I checked in on Griffin, Wild Thing, Peter Seeger and Philip Seymour Hoffman. I found them at Griffin's Cave. Peter Seeger was still sitting on his stool in the field of flowers singing, "If I had a hammer..." Philip Seymour Hoffman was lying on the ground in front of the cave listening to Seeger singing and playing his banjo. Griffin was next to him, part way in his cave and part way out of the cave. Wild Thing was next to Griffin sitting down on the ground with a big smile and holding his banjo in his left hand. I put my hand on Griffin's hind leg. He didn't turn to see what it was but acknowledged my presence with a swish of his tail. I waved my hand at Peter Seeger. He acknowledged my arrival with a nod of his head and began to sing "Michael Row The Boat Ashore ...Hallelujah..." I took this as a positive sign of approval, since my name is Michael and I left them all alone enjoying the music.

The next night I returned looking for Griffin. First, I went to his cave, but no one was there. I finally found him wondering around alone in the darkness. He was injured and unable to fly. I asked him what had happened and where were the others. Griffin told me that he was attacked by what sounded to me like a saber tooth tiger. They are, after all, living deep in the past before there were any real humans around. I gave Griffin a dose of magic potion that can heal any injury and cure any illness. He responded immediately to the magic in the medicine. Then, we went in search of the other three. Griffin said he had left them in the tiger's den. He said that the cave had been too small for him to get inside and that was where he was attacked from above while they were investigating the cave.

When we finally reached the cave, we found that Seeger had badly injured his left hand, while trying to escape from the tiger. Seymour and Wild Thing were frightened but unharmed. The same magic potion I used for Griffin, I also used to treat Seeger's injuries. He too experienced a rapid magical recovery and could once again play his banjo.

It took us most of the rest of the night to make our way through unfamiliar terrain, in darkness, back to Griffin's Cave. I left them there at the cave, near the field of flowers with Seeger once again singing and playing his banjo. Before I took my leave, I built a bonfire to keep wild animals away. "Feed the fire until I return" I warned them.

From there, I returned to Never Land to see if it would be possible to transport the magic fire pit that Baldwin had built back to Griffin's cave. It was quite an undertaking but I finally managed to transport the fire pit to where the Griffin's cave had been located, then I transported it back through time to when and where the four of them were staying. Since a griffin is a magical creature, it seemed like a good possibility that I could show Griffin how to use the magical fire pit, to create a never-ending fire, so they would not need to constantly refuel the fire with more and more wood. Griffin quickly learned the process of lighting and extinguishing the fire pit. I left them with a good defense to protect them while they slept and a means of staying warm in winter.

The Night Bus

The night before last, at 2:11 a.m., my wife said to me, "There is something here." Things almost always come to her side of the bed. That may be because the doorway to our bedroom is nearer to her side of the bed. Perhaps it is because I would probably just sleep through 'whatever' anyway. She always wants to know the same thing from me. She always wants to know what it is, why it is there, and how fast I can get rid of whatever it is.

I looked over near the doorway next to the bed and this is what I saw: There was this thin, tan-colored rabbit, about five feet tall, who was wearing a plaid flannel, long-sleeve shirt with the sleeves rolled half way up his fore arms. He wore blue denim jeans with the cuffs rolled up several times because the pant legs were too long. His very long ears hung down sadly beside his face. He held his soft straw hat in his furry paws, nervously twisting and rolling its brim. I asked if he were Peter Rabbit since he had that soft pastel look of a Beatrix Potter creation. He gave me a long, soft, slow, "Noooo...." Then I asked if he were Roger Rabbit. He again replied with a long, soft, slow, "Nooo..." "Well, who are you and why are you here and what do you want?" I said.

He told me his name was Waldo and he had missed the bus. I of course wanted to know what bus? He said that he had missed the Night Bus.

I asked Waldo where he needed to be. He said that

he needed to be in Wichita, Kansas by the 20th of March. I asked him how he managed to get to my house in the first place. He told me that he drove his truck. It was out in front of the house but it wouldn't start. I went out with him and checked the truck out to see if it could be fixed without too much trouble. It appeared to be a 1946 model something. In the dark, it was difficult to determine if it were a Ford, a Chevy, or some other make. The red paint on the cab was badly faded from over exposure to sun and wind and rain and snow and to too much time itself. The bed was flat and made of oak planking that was old and well worn. It had removable wooden railing on the front, back and sides for hauling hay or boxes or maybe even cows

Under the hood, I noticed that the coil wire had come out of the coil. I replaced it and asked Waldo to give it a try. He sheepishly admitted that he had run the battery all the way down while trying to get the truck started. I gave him a jump from my car and got him on his way.

I rode with him for more than half an hour just to make sure he was headed in the right direction and on the right road. The hard flat bench seat in the rabbit's truck reminded me of 'Old 20,' the flat bed truck that my father drove when I was about eight years old. They called it 'Old Twenty' because the truck was very old and it had a twenty-foot long bed. My dad would sometimes take me with him on those long trips to deliver equipment or materials for the construction company he worked for. There was no radio, no air conditioning and a heater that worked very poorly. The windows were always open. My dad smoked his Camel cigarettes constantly. There was a canvas water bag swinging from the side mirror, kept cool by the onrushing wind. The constant drone of the diesel engine always lulled me to sleep. There was little conversation possible because of the loud hammering diesel and the wind constantly howling through the open windows.

As we drove down the road, everything illuminated in the dim bouncing light from the antique headlights was from the past, from the late forty's to the early fifty's, no later than 1951, when I was eight years old. The roads were mostly dirt. The cars were all very old and the houses small and quaint. I asked Waldo Rabbit what I looked like to him. Waldo said that I was a freckled-faced little boy, eight years old, wearing a plaid flannel shirt and dirty blue jeans and my hair was all messed up.

The next night at 2:20 a.m., my wife rolled over, grabbed my arm and said, "Something is here!" I looked over to her side of the bed and sure enough, there was this big fat raccoon with a dark brown leather cap pulled down low over his eyes. He wore a dark gray leather vest absent any buttons, faded black pants and a long sleeve shirt. He was shorter than Waldo Rabbit by half a foot. He stood barely four feet tall. I abruptly said, "Who are you and what do you want?"

The raccoon was very grouchy. He gruffly replied, "I'm Brad Coon. I'm the driver of the Night Bus. Where is Waldo Rabbit? I came to pick him up. I'm already running late." I told Brad Coon, the Night Bus Driver, that Waldo Rabbit had problems with the coil on his truck but he left here last night after I helped him get his old truck running.

The bus driver abruptly turned around as he mumbled to himself, beneath his breath, "I hope he makes it back by the 20th." And then he was gone.

Speaking of Foxes

Recently, while speaking with foxes, the need arose to query one's impending death. The event horizon seemed to be an appropriate starting point to thusly converse. I summoned the death of the Fox from its unseen future. Slowly they approached from the horizon, with Death at the tiller, with Death at the pole. Death slowly pushed their raft into the present, with one pole and with one push at a time. The Fox and its Death eventually arrived at the edge of the water where the sand sloped up to meet the beach where I was standing.

Death was a young African male with long curly dread locks and very light skin. He wore only a loincloth and held the Fox tightly with one hand allowing very little freedom for the Fox to move.

I asked Fox's death why he felt the need to constantly restrain the Fox since they traveled life together on such a small raft in such a large ocean. He had no answer. We talked at great length about his responsibilities as the Death of the Fox. It took a great deal of logic and a great deal of discourse to convince the Fox's Death that it really wasn't necessary to hold the Fox so tightly that it would imprison the Fox. Imprisonment was not one of Death's assignments. Only the punctuality and propriety of death were needed.

Eventually Fox's Death relented and agreed to allow Fox the freedom of movement on their raft in exchange for her not dithering at the time of death's toll. They left together as partners in life and in death and they slowly rafted their way back into the future and disappeared into the event horizon.

Though this story is presented as an allegory, it is the representation of a real person and their actual situation, where their death was preventing them from having freedom of choice with respect to having any normalcy in the time left for them here in this life, in this reality. My intervention in no way altered the time or the place or any specific details of the Fox's future death but only the freedom for Fox to resume living freed from that constant, unrelenting threat of its imminent death.

Though this intervention may alter future choices that the Fox makes it is not an example of the butterfly effect but merely an example of the use of the event horizon in a constructive way to modify the Fox's perception and return to Fox her freedom of choice.

The Strings of Consternation

All events come with strings attached. The more closely you scrutinize these strings the more aware you become of their interconnectivity. All events are connected at some level. There are no co-incidences only voids in our awareness of how intimately events are all intertwined. This is an attempt to present a personal example of existing relationships between seemingly disparate events.

Please review related columns in conjunction with today's allegory. Several months ago, a lady presented at my office seeking specific health care. Our practice is basically limited to special needs patients and children with behavioral issues or complex health issues. When an adult, who is not flagged as a special needs patient, presents their self for care at my office, the first question that enters my mind is, "Why are you here? There are more than one hundred providers in the city that could provide you with appropriate care."

I had been working diligently every day for more than a month, on understanding how the event horizon actually functions but I was making little progress.

This prospective patient reminded me of my third grade teacher, Mrs. Duncan. She wore the same style of glasses, had the same hairstyle, the same complexion, the same features, the same physical build and she even had the same unusual scar on one cheek. I had a strong feeling that she was looking for a place to die and I didn't want it to be on my watch. This extreme level of concern motivated me to finally acquire a working knowledge of the event horizon.

Acquiring a basic understanding of what a boundary layer vortex is and how it can function as a time tunnel into the past or into the future, resulted in my return to the past, to a time and age of eight years and six or eighths months.

That was when Mrs. Duncan was my third grade teacher.

That was when our overly large third grade class was divided into two third grade classes and I lost my teacher, Mrs. Duncan.

That was when I stopped loving my teachers.

That was when I left childhood behind.

I went back in time through the boundary layer vortex to where and when Mrs. Duncan was, when I was an eight-year old child. I went back to the day I was leaving her class. She pinched me on the cheek, my right cheek, the cheek with a scar like hers and she said to me "If you ever need me, I'll be there for you" and she was. That venture into the past opened a doorway back into my childhood and it brought the Night Bus, just as my journey in the opposite direction, into the future through the vortex, opened a doorway for Zephyrs to come through, from another dimension, back in time, back into our time and into our dimension.

Izzy, Izzy...Izzy?

It was late, or early, depending on how you think of late and early. It was about 1:30 in the morning. There was something on the floor next to my bed that was reaching up and trying to get on to the bed but it was having a hard time of it because it was only about eleven inches tall. I thought about the situation but just for a moment, before I put my arm over the side of the bed and allowed the creature to clamber up onto the top of the bed next to my pillow.

I was staring into the face of what looked exactly like a Smurf, down to the smallest detail. It was blue. It had an enormous droopy hat. It had that dumb cartoonish face. I certainly didn't think a Smurf posed any threat to me. Then I began my inquiry. "Are you a Smurf? You look like a Smurf. Can you talk? Do you speak English? Do you communicate telepathically?" I was greeted with its blank stare. Then I put on the rose-colored glasses which allow me to see things as they really are, as opposed to how they might appear to be.

This creature then, looked nothing like a Smurf. It was very skinny. It had only two fingers on each hand. It was basically a luminous outline, with no body and no substance. At that moment, I moved my right arm, the arm I had allowed the creature to use to climb up onto the bed. I was shocked. I felt a great pain in my elbow. I knew that this creature had something to do with the pain in my arm. I took out my 'Sword of Truth' and placed its point directly in front of the creature's nose or where a nose should have been and said, "You did something to my elbow. You better fix it or I'm going to chop your head off." As the pain began to dissipate, the creature began to shrink. I found out from the creature that it was an Izzy and fed on the pain of others. The more I prodded it, the more the pain left my elbow and the smaller the Izzy became.

When the last remnants of pain disappeared, the Izzy vanished into a shower of tiny bubbles, which were, I suppose, its seeds of sorrow or spores for tomorrow or something to that effect.

So, is a Smurf an Izzy, or is an Izzy an Izzy, or is an Izzy, not?

Being pragmatic and being a utilitarian, I wondered, if someone were to have pain of unknown origin, with the absence of inflammation, could there actually be an Izzy involved. If so, should one seek assistance from a medicine man or from a wizard or perhaps even a sorcerer, a person of mystery and magic, someone who would know if there were an Izzy and how to get rid of it, if there were.

Worry-za-waste

I was actively engaged in thinking about all of the issues that had transpired that day instead of going to sleep. There were so many unresolved and unresolvable issues floating around inside of my head. I was tossing and turning. Then my wife said, "Is there something here?"

I stopped my futile activity and focused on the possibility that something might, in fact, be roaming around inside of our bedroom. I scanned the entire room but saw nothing. I put on the rose-colored glasses and again, I saw nothing. Then I drew the shimmering sword. There in its reflection, I saw two shining eyes and a monkey-like creature hanging from the ceiling near the doorway. I followed it as it came across the ceiling towards me, dropped onto the floor next to me, then clambered onto the bed and was trying to lick me with its long pointed tongue. I held it at bay with my left hand and squeezed its neck harder and harder. As I did so, little bubbles began to appear all over its body. The harder I squeezed the monkey's neck, the more bubbles formed on it, until the creature was completely overcome by the weight of these bubbles and it gave up trying to lick me and hobbled out of the bedroom, laden with the weight of baby Izzys.

Later when I asked the Source if this creature was attracted to worry, he laughed and retorted, "Worry-za-waste."

Salis Burry

I always take my Cardigan Welsh Corgi out to the back yard for his final duty about eight o'clock at night. He roams around the yard finding new spots and new smells before he retires for the evening but not tonight. Instead of rushing headlong into the bushes, he stopped dead in his tracks like a pointer hound, instead of a herder Corgi. He only made it half way down the cool deck beside the pool before he froze stiff, unwilling or unable to take another step forward. I passed by him, calling back for him to come with me several times as I moved out into the darkness and on around the entire pool. He remained frozen, unmoving, with eyes fixed into the darkness on something I couldn't see. Not until I entered the house did he slowly turn and creep back inside.

My wife told me that Jeremy, our pet bird, would not come out of his cage. He hadn't been out of his cage for three days. He normally comes out as soon as his cage door is opened and follows the dog around or takes a bath in the dog's bowl of water or makes a nuisance of himself. Instead of flying out of his cage at the first opportunity, he huddled in the corner of his cage muttering to himself. I told my wife that something had to be out there, somewhere in the darkness.

The first thing I did, after we turned the lights off, was to locate the Facilitator and the child who were sitting on the park bench staring into the bank of fog leading into the event horizon. I sat down between them and shared my concern raised by our Corgi and Jeremy the family Crow. It was suggested that I attempt to discover what was out there, in the future, by going into the fog bank by myself. If I felt that additional resources were deemed appropriate, then I was to request assistance.

I walked slowly, deep into the fog, until I could feel the ocean on my feet. I stopped, opened a window into the fog and then calmed the surface of the water that was exposed. In the distance, at the edge of the event horizon, a door opened and a nicely dressed young man, with dark, neatly-trimmed hair, stepped out. He was not quite six feet tall. He came towards me with a long confident stride. I said in a loud clear voice, "Who are you, what do you want?"

He hesitated, then stated that his name was Salis Burry and he had come for all of the animals that I had. I asked what animals was he talking about. He said that he had come for the three bears and the three lions and the four unicorns and any other magical creatures that were in Never Land. "Why would I do that?" I said. He raised both of his arms as high as he could, then said that he was sent by a powerful sorcerer to bring all of the magical creatures that I had, back to him.

I summoned the Facilitator who appeared on my left side as a huge lion. I summoned the Other who appeared on my right side as a luminous double of myself. Then, unannounced, the child emerged out of the fog bank beside me, took the Oakenthor from his pocket and pointed it at the intruder. A stream of what looked like electricity flew from the small gold Oakenthor and attached itself to the young man. He was incinerated, spinning rapidly on the surface of the water like fat in a frying pan. Then he disappeared in a puff of smoke.

I asked the Facilitator what that was all about. He said, "When you have a coming out from hiding, like you have done and announce your presence, others will begin to attack you and try to take anything they can away from you. That particular sorcerer believes his power is derived from the magical creatures that he dominates but that is untrue.

I took out a magical arrow shaft, attached a message to it, fitted its knock to the leather string of my magical bow and drew the four foot arrow with its bronze tip to its fullest. I released it with full knowledge that it passed through time and space and dimensions and realities until it sank deep into that Sorcerer's mantle above his fireplace with a loud crash. The message unfurled. In Latin, it read, "in oculi, in oculorum!

Startled, he grabbed its shaft firmly to pull it out from his wooden mantle. He screamed in pain as the shaft glowed red hot, permanently branding his skin. Next, he drew his magic wand, attempted to use it to dislodge the arrow shaft with its haunting message but that resulted in his chandelier crashing to the floor, shattering in a shower of glass shards. He tried one last time and that resulted with a large hole blasting through his slate roof. The magic arrow shaft with its message remains unscathed protruding from the sorcerer's mantle for all to see, a monument in Latin to his arrogance.

Boundary Layer Vortex

A few days ago the Facilitator told me that I was ready to be introduced to the boundary layer vortex. I told the Facilitator that I'm always ready for any adventure. He extended his hand to me and said, "Don't let go!"

We proceeded to the very edge of our dimension, the third dimension, where it comes in contact with an adjacent dimension. I don't know if we were next to the second dimension or next to the fourth dimension.

There are seven dimensions in our universe. I'm not sure if there are seven dimensions in the parallel universe but for sure there is a parallel universe. I know because I have been there. The seven dimensions are strung together in a curving, distorted S-shape. I have made it to all seven dimensions but I have only spent a significant amount of time in the second dimension. Each dimension has its own peculiar properties. Time in the second dimension is approximately eighteen times as slow as time is in our dimension. Things happen in super-slow motion.

The boundary layer I am referring to here is where two different time systems from two different adjacent dimensions come into close proximity to each other, thereby creating a vortex. This vortex is essentially a 'time tornado'. It is the entryway into a wormhole, a wormhole in time, through which one can travel into the future or back into the past.

I know of four different techniques for traveling

through time. This one is new to me, so I don't yet know its strengths or its weaknesses. I assume the greater the difference between time systems, the greater the existing energy potential but that may prove to be a moot point.

This process involves the following steps: First you must get to the edge of our dimension. Second, you must get to that point which is in close proximity to another dimension with a different time system. Third, you must locate the time vortex being created and then you must jump into the center of that vortex. This is all quite new to me, so I am not exactly sure what determines where and when you will emerge but I do know that you should try to re-enter the same worm hole at the other side for a safe return to our time and our dimension.

The act of jumping into the vortex apparently opens the wormhole. I don't know what keeps the wormhole open. I don't know how long the passageway through time thus created stays open. I don't know how stable the whole system is and I have no idea how to close this gateway to another time or if it just closes up on its own or if it remains open.

Trial and error is fraught with unknown risks but in this arena, it is often the only option. In my world, it is watch one, do one, teach one. Thus I tried this process for the first time on my own but this time I went into the future instead of into the past. The difference between traveling into the future, instead of traveling into the past, is that you must find a vortex that is spinning in the opposite direction that is clockwise. When I went into the past, I grew younger and younger, until I was nine years old. That was sixty-two years into the past. When I went into the future, I grew older and older until I was ninety-five and getting soft in the head. I stopped there because I didn't want to return a dead man or maybe to not return at all but perhaps become a carcass, floating, lost somewhere in time.

Zephyr

I was watching the Academy Awards when my son who lives in California called. He said that there was something at his house and he wanted me to come over and check it out. I asked what he thought it was and where it was located. He told me that it felt something like a cloud over his house. Any information can be helpful in locating and dealing with whatever an issue is.

Later, after the Academy Awards program was over, I prepared to go check out the situation. First I decide whether to go it alone or, if I should take someone along with me for the adventure. I recently established a connection with my death, so I asked Robert if he wanted to accompany me on this adventure. Since his primary responsibility is to keep me alive, it seemed like I would be hedging my bet.

We arrived in my son's back yard uneventfully. One never knows what could happen when traveling through different portals with your death. I checked out the area above his roof carefully. There was a large array above his roof consisting of translucent tubes arranged in an oval shape like the track around a football field but smaller in size. It was less than one hundred feet long and maybe forty feet wide. The perimeter was made of a single tube that was transected longitudinally by another tube. Five other tubes that were all attached at ninety-degree angles to it transected this tube. These attached to the sides of the oval. The two vertical tubes that were attached at each end of the oval supported this entire array. They were attached to the roof of his house. These tubes were all the same size, and appeared to be made of some synthetic material. The diameter of each tube was not more than 5/8 of an inch, about 14 millimeters. I looked all around the yard but since I had no idea what this thing was or what I should do with it, I decided to leave for now and come back later.

I went back to California a little later but this time I took the Facilitator with me. He and I have a very long history together. He is very powerful and quite capable of dealing with all kinds of unknown situations. I asked him if he had ever seen anything like this structure before. He told me that he had no idea what it was or what to do with it. I told the Facilitator that this thing had to go, no matter what it was or where it came from. I set an explosive pulse generating charge in the middle of the array. We vacated the premises and detonated the device. It broke into several pieces but the pieces didn't disappear, so I knew that this array had some physical properties, even though they were very difficult to see visibly. We again left but returned about an hour later.

When we arrived this time, there was a strange, almost insect-like creature in the back yard next to the swimming pool. It had eight appendages that looked very much like the tubing from the now defunct array. There were six legs attached to a horizontal body and two arms attached to a vertical torso. It had two large bulging eyes but no neck or head. The two eyes were attached to the uppermost, rounded end of the torso. The whole thing appeared very mechanical and robotic to me. When I put on the rose-colored glasses, the tubing changed from pale, translucent, ice-blue to a multicolor arrangement of tubing. I drew the magical short sword to observe the thing's reflection from the swords mirror surface to see what it really looked like. The image reflected from the gleaming surface of the sword had the tubing completely fleshed out in shimmering colors and made it appear even more like an insect. When I drew the sword, this creature, which was taller than me, stopped in its tracks.

I spent some time trying to communicate with this creature. After a great deal of effort, the creature began to communicate telepathically. I of course wanted to know what it was, where it came from, how it got here, what it was doing with that array of tubing, as well as many other things.

This is what I found out. This thing is called a Zephyr. It came from the fifth dimension. It came from the future. The array was gathering what it called iridescence. Whatever that is, I'm not sure but I think it has something to do with some quality of time or some form of energy. When I asked how it managed to get here, the Zephyr told me that they, now it was they, had come through a time portal, the time portal which I had inadvertently left open. I was totally shocked.

Last week, the Facilitator had told me that he thought I was ready to be introduced to an alternate method of time travel. He took me to the edge of our dimension that is the third dimension, where it comes very close to the fourth dimension that has a different speed at which time moves. The difference in speeds of time between the two different dimensions creates eddy currents and when they are close enough, become a twirling vortex that can be turned into a time portal through which physical objects can be transported.

He took me back in time sixty-two years, with plates of food, to demonstrate how to modify the vortex and convert it into an open time portal through which people and objects can travel. The problem with this method was that my own age was simultaneously altered by sixty-two years as well.

A couple of days later, I tried to duplicate this process by opening a time portal and going into the future. Apparently I didn't pay close enough attention to the details and had left the time portal open.

By the time I returned my attention to the creature, a second Zephyr had emerged sopping wet from the swimming pool and was moving towards me. I told them that they had to get out of there and take their junk with them or they would get stuck here permanently because I was going to close the portal. Then I left again.

When I returned the next time, I drew the magical sword, made my way to the open portal and pop, first one Zephyr disappeared and then a second and finally a third Zephyr along with their array of tubing disappeared into the time portal. I stuck the blade of the sword crosswise into the edge of the swirling portal and the vortex slowed down further and further until it stopped and the portal to the fifth dimension and the future closed.

During the period of days when the portal to the future was open, weird things were happening, all related to some sort of time distortion, a 'Wrinkle in Time.'

I returned to my son's house a fifth and final time to make sure everything was indeed back to normal but five trips over to California in one night was quite a lot, even for a sorcerer like me.

Beware... Beware

Last night I was awake before 2:00 a.m. so I went out to catch the Night Bus. I climbed on board and asked Brad, the bus driver, if he could take me to the tenth attention, a place I had never been to before. The bus started moving slowly down the street then it began to stutter along before eventually stopping at the tenth attention. Brad opened the doors to the bus before saying, "Beware" then again as I stepped off of the bus, "Beware." In all my many adventures with the bus driver, Brad has never told me to "Beware".

The air was heavy and humid. It was dark but not black, dark like fog at twilight. Since I had never been to the tenth attention before, I had no idea what to expect and after two beware warnings I decided to stay put and to not move until I had some idea of what was going on. With the rose-colored glasses I could detect movement but nothing else. With the double-lensed pince-nez spectacles I could detect shapes but I was unable to tell what the shapes were. With the reflections from the Sword of Truth, I could see human forms devoid of any details, no hair or faces or ears or fingers, just moving outlines of human forms enshrouded in skintight garments like Spider Man. I could not even be sure of the gender of the moving shapes. One of the forms stopped in front of me. As my point of focus moved above this human shape, the face of a woman appeared. Her hair was unkempt. It appeared to be dirty and matted, medium length and dark brown. Her skin was olive in complexion. She appeared to be in her late thirties or early forties. I was unable to establish direct communication with her. The next form that appeared in front of me was that of a child. I looked above it and the face of a young man perhaps in his early twenties appeared. His skin was covered in pimples and his hair was long for a boy. It was a very dark brown and it was also matted and dirty.

The face did not match the form of the small child that stood before me, yet I knew that they were somehow connected.

A third form appeared before me briefly. When I focused my attention above this shape, the face of an adult male appeared. He needed a shave. His hair was receding and speckled with gray. It was medium to short in length and in need of cutting. Each of these three forms and their faces had their story to tell. I just didn't know how to communicate with them so they could share their tales. Next time I hope to do better.

The next night I again caught the Night Bus and asked to return to the tenth attention. Brad, the bus driver squinted his disapproval through his beady little raccoon eyes. Once again the driver warned me, not once but twice, as I was leaving the bus when we arrived at the tenth attention, "Beware…Beware".

This time I established that each one of these three individuals had done something and then ended up here in this strange place. But, I never found out what it was that landed them here.

I queried the Source about the tenth attention and about the people that were there. He didn't provide me with any useful information. But, the Source also warned me two times, "Beware… Beware". He has never warned me about anything before. His warnings seemed more ominous.

The next night I returned to the tenth attention but this time I went by portal instead of by Night Bus. When I entered the tenth attention, I entered above this sea of dark gray fog. Above the fog was what we would think of as air. I could see clearly for a long distance. Something was moving across the surface of the sea of fog but I couldn't see what it was. When I plunged beneath the surface of the dense fog, I could sense some kind of capturing device like a net or hook and line that was moving back and forth through the dense fog in a random pattern apparently in an effort to capture or hook one of these human forms that were moving around and drag them up to the surface for some unknown purpose.

Since I was unable to see either the capturing device or the thing that was trying to capture one of these human forms, I decided to heed the warnings from Brad the bus driver and the Source and I took my leave of the tenth attention before I became somehow ensnared there in that place.

Later, the Source said, "Michael, walk with me." He held his hands clasped together behind his back as we walked slowly with no apparent destination in mind. He looked down as though contemplating how and what exactly he was willing to share with me. The Source told me that each of these human forms was permanently imprisoned in the tenth attention by their own choices. It was impossible for them to extricate themselves from the tenth attention. He said that the faces that appeared were the faces of the individuals who were still alive. The human forms contained the encased spirits and attention of those individuals rendering them zombie-like. The three forms that I encountered close up and in person had all been there in the tenth attention for fourteen years.

I asked the Source if there were any way I could get them out of there. He told me that the only reason that I myself had not been captured by these creatures living there in the tenth attention was that I had come of my own free will and I had come as a pin-point of awareness, making it impossible for them to detect my presence. I asked if it were possible for me to assist them in some way. He said, "All things are possible... but this, is very improbable."

I took him at his word and left well enough alone... at least for the time being.

Canary Road

Last night I was conversing with the Source when he told me he thought that it was time for me to return to the tenth attention and rescue those unfortunate souls hopelessly trapped there and unable to escape.

I reminded the Source that he had warned me to, "Beware...beware" and told me that it was not possible for me to help the people trapped there in the tenth attention. Later he reiterated that it was a hopeless situation.

Now all of a sudden he wanted me not only to go back to the tenth attention but also to rescue all those people hopelessly stranded there. The most bizarre thing about those trapped there was that they were all alive but their minds were entrapped in the tenth attention. They were for all practical purposes real live zombies.

After the Source asked me to go to the tenth attention and rescue all those hopelessly trapped spirits he departed leaving me to work through his request and create a successful strategy.

The first thing I did was to ask the Facilitator what he thought about me going to the tenth attention to rescue all of those zombie spirits trapped there. He thought that it was a very bad idea and told me not to go. Next I asked Sabatini the traveler's Buddha what he thought about me going there. He also thought it was a bad idea to go there and advised me not to go. Then I asked the wizard's elf what he thought about going to the tenth attention. He said there was no way he was going to go there and then vanished from sight. The last person I asked was the wizard's giant. He said he would go, no questions asked. I told him that the night bus would be coming soon but he would have to ride on the bus, not in the bus because he was so large. The giant said that it wouldn't be a problem for him to ride on the bus instead of in it.

But, subsequently I decided that there would be too much unknown risk if I took anyone with me. I needed to go alone. I also didn't want to risk losing any of the many 'tools' I had collected through the years. So, I went with nothing but the leather thong that Aru the Aborigine keeper of Dream Time had given me as a gift years ago.

The Night Bus arrived a few minutes later. When I climbed on board Brad the bus driver gave me a weird look. I asked Brad what he was hauling on the Night Bus today. He told me canaries. The bus was full of yellow canaries. They were everywhere. I asked Brad where he was taking all these canaries. He said, to the coalmines. I asked him why he was taking all these pretty yellow canaries to the coalmines where it was dark and dirty. Brad said that when the canaries dropped dead, the coal miners knew it was time for them to get out of the mines because there was methane gas present. It was invisible, odorless and deadly and they had to get out of there in a hurry or they too would die.

When I told the bus driver that I needed to go to the tenth attention, he said, with a frown on his face, that he would drop the birds off first and then take me to the tenth attention. I told the canaries that if they went with the bus driver Brad to the coalmines they were all doomed to die a terrible death but if they went with me to the tenth attention there was a chance that they might survive. They all decided to take their chances with me much to the bus driver's consternation. As we made our way to the tenth attention, I asked Brad how many canaries were on the bus. My guess was about ten thousand. He said there were twelve thousand yellow male canaries. Those are the ones that sing constantly. They were all making so much racket that I told them if they wanted me to try to save them, they would have to follow my orders and do exactly as I said. My first order was for them to be quiet. When we arrived at the tenth attention I told the canaries to stay together and wait there for me while I surveyed the situation from above where all the humans were trapped, to see what was trying to catch them.

There were three giant creatures dredging with their long curved fingernails that were concave and would hook and scoop up the human spirits that were thrashing around hopelessly beneath the surface of what we might think of as a shallow sea. These creatures were hundreds of feet tall. I really needed to think up a scheme and think it up fast before we all would become lost souls in this dreadful place.

The Source has asked me to do many seemingly impossible things when he thought I was ready. He never told me how to accomplish these tasks but he always provided the things needed to get the job done but it was always up to me to figure out the puzzle before my time had run out. How could these puny yellow canaries save the day because I was no match for these three giant creatures with nothing but a leather thong.

Eureka! Then I made the connection. The source used the term hopeless several times in reference to these lost souls. They had all put themselves into the tenth attention by the decisions that they had made and it was hopeless for them to get out by themselves. That was it. That was the answer.

Miners in a coalmine were all hopelessly doomed to die from deadly methane gas. Their only hope came from these little yellow canaries. When the canaries stopped singing it was time to get out of the mines. These tiny yellow songsters would bring the gift of hope to these hopelessly lost souls. I told the canaries to each go to one of the people there and sing them their song and as they did so, each of the people vanished and returned to the world of the living to resume their lives. They were no longer zombies but normal functioning people. These puny little yellow canaries had given them hope.

Rainy Day

The rain woke me. I had never ventured outside to stand in the rain in the middle of the night. I assumed that the experience would be somewhat familiar to me but it wasn't. I couldn't feel the raindrops hitting my face or hands. The drops were quite large but appeared to be two dimensional and floated down like large snowflakes. When I put on the rose-colored glasses the floating feathery raindrops appeared to puff up and blossomed into red-tinted balls of fluff. With the pince-nez spectacles on they looked more like large fluttery fish-scales. In the reflection from the shiny surface of the 'sword of truth' the raindrops appeared to be floating discs of light.

It was like driving your dirty car with muddy windows into a car wash. The raindrops washed away the mud and dirt allowing me to see things clearly. When I looked at my hand there was only a thin thread of blue that outlined where my transparent hand remained.

Later I asked the Source about the raindrop experience. He said that the experience with the lava, on Mount Etna, had burned away any remaining remnants of my human form and the raindrops of pure water had washed away the soot from my vision so that now I could see clearly for the first time. The only remaining thing required of me now was to go 'into the light' which I did. After I did that, I told the Source that the light didn't seem to do anything.

The Source told me to go into the bathroom and to look at my reflection in the mirror. I did so. I had no reflection. The source said that I had been purified and completely cleansed of 'the human form'. It was now possible for me to go anywhere in the blink of an eye. I could now travel into the past or into the future or to any location instantaneously no matter how far, without leaving a single trace. I would no longer create any disturbance to the future, the past or any other place by having been there, I could travel effortlessly even to the depths of Hell or other dimensions without being detected and without ill effects. I tried it and it works.

I went to visit the Oracle. He lives some twenty-seven hundred years in the past. When I ventured into the cave, I illuminated his cavern with light from the golden disc. It appears like the moonlight from a full moon but there is no moon. When I approached the Oracle, he said, "Is that you, Michael? I see the moonlight but I can't see you, for you have no presence and the moonlight has no source."

Door to Tomorrow

The full moon came on the twelfth day in the month of June. No crows came in the morning, after midnight. I thought they would probably come that evening before midnight. It was after eleven thirty in the evening before I could go looking for the magic crows. My plane had arrived late. I was visiting my son in California for Father's Day. I assumed the crows would come here to California. I went outside to the front of his house and outside to the back of his house but there were no crows to be found in either place. It was getting late and the crows need to be gone by midnight on the day of the full moon, so I took the portal back to my home in Arizona. Sure enough, those crows were waiting for me there in my own back yard.

There were five of them that formed a semi-circle, in front of me. A sixth crow came out of the darkness and handed me an odd-shaped antique key strung on a necklace of tiny silver beads. The magic crow told me that this was the key to the Door to Tomorrow. As soon as he handed me the key, all of the crows scattered in every direction and disappeared into the night sky just before midnight arrived.

I was really tired from the flight over to California, so I put the necklace around my neck and went to sleep. I woke up at four in the morning and decided to check out the gift from the magic crows. The key itself was really bizarre. The top looked like an antique old key with an open cloverleaf pattern. The center of the round shaft had a small hourglass-shaped thickened portion. The business end of the key had three different elements protruding like a tripod from its tip. There was an open circle, a zigzag thing, like a bolt of lightning and a small curved blade with a rounded tip. I had never seen anything remotely like it before. I had no idea how it could possibly work.

I asked the Facilitator if he was interested in going with me to look for this 'Door to Tomorrow. He declined as well did a lot of other potential partners for this adventure. Finally, I got Philip, the magic horse, and the 'Other', to accompany me on this quest.

Getting to the 'Door to Tomorrow' was pretty simple. We took the portal and were there in no time. The Door to Tomorrow was a huge metal door with no hinges, no doorknob, and no keyhole, just the words, 'DOOR TO TOMORROW', writ large on its front. I ran my fingers around the edges of the door but there was no space between the door and the stonewall encasing it.

The chief crow had said that this was the key to the Door to Tomorrow. I sat down on the ground in front of the huge metal door and gave it some thought. Then I put on the double-lens pince-nez glasses that are supposed to allow me to see things as they really are. I assumed that the bolt of lightning part of the key, represented energy of some kind. I also assumed that the circle represented the full moon, which was still shining. I asked the 'Other,' which is composed of pure energy, to touch the door. The metal door lit up immediately and a circle appeared on its surface. I touched the circle but nothing happened. Then, I remembered the small blade on the end of the key that reminded me of the blade on a quick knife used to clean the bottom of a horse hoof before a horseshoe is nailed into place. I asked Philip, the magic horse, to put his hoof on top of the circle on the door. The door became transparent and shimmered like hot air from a mirage in the desert heat and we walked through the doorway together, into 'Tomorrow'.

At the End of the Rainbow

When I was little, my Father would tell me there was a pot of gold at the end of the rainbow every time we saw one. That was rare living in the Sonoran Desert. Last night I was awake when it was time for the red and black biplane to pass over, so I waited out on the curb under the street light in front of our house in hopes of catching a ride. I heard the faint rumble coming from the approaching airplane. The sound dropped off sharply. I knew it was coming in for a direct approach landing. Moments later, it touched down gently at the far end of our street. The engine fell silent as the propeller spun down. The old biplane rolled silently to a stop directly in front of my driveway. I asked the pilot if he could take me to the pot of gold at the end of the rainbow. The Poodle scratched his wrinkled brow for a moment, before shaking his head up and down with an affirmative gesture. He motioned with his twirling paw for me to give the prop a pull. I signaled him with a kill sign to make sure the magneto was off before I approached the oversized wooden propeller with its tarnished brass leading edge. I pulled the propeller through slowly until one cylinder was positioned just before top dead center. I gave him the thumbs up so he could turn the magneto back on and I gave the prop a big pull. The engine popped and sputtered to life, rattling and shaking the spruce and wire structure of the rickety airframe. I clambered up into the front hole and we were off on another adventure, heading for the end of the rainbow.

It was barely 1:00 o'clock in the morning and quite dark outside. Before long it was twilight and we were flying low over what looked like Ireland, with its lush green landscape. We sat down roughly in a fairly level pasture near a dense forest, with a beautiful rainbow coming down out of the clouds just beyond. I jumped out and thanked the pilot before running into the forest in search of the rainbow's end. The forest opened abruptly at the edge of a deep, wide abyss. On the other side was a huge iron pot with the rainbow emerging from it. I had no idea how I could possibly get across the precipice. I shouted into the canyon all of the names of leprechauns that I knew. Each name echoed back to me in turn, to no avail but a rope bridge magically appeared that crossed over to the other side of the gorge. At its entrance, stood a little old leprechaun wearing an emerald green stovepipe hat, and matching bright green wool vest. I ran over to him and asked if I could cross over the chasm on his swaying rope bridge. He looked up at me, squinted his beady little eyes until they were almost closed and asked, "What is the magic word?" I replied, "I believe!" He removed his tall hat quickly and bowed so low that his nose almost touched the grass. I made my way across the swaying rope bridge to the other side and on to where the giant iron pot sat, with the rainbow bubbling up out of it.

Several leprechauns were running around the boiling pot feeding the fire at its base with dry twigs and leaves and even some pieces of old rope discarded from a worn-out bridge. Inside the huge cauldron was molten gold bubbling away, its vapors were condensing into the shimmering rainbow of colors arching across the sky towards the clouds in the distance. It was obvious that there was a pot of gold at the end of the rainbow but there was no way I could take any of the molten metal back with me.

I made my way back across the hemp rope bridge and back to my bedroom. The clock beside my bed displayed 1:20 a.m. in large red numerals. It had taken only twenty minutes to go and to come back. The only evidence left of my adventure was the brown stains on my fingers from crossing the rope bridge and the lingering smell of burning hemp rope still hanging in my bedroom.

Hope is Not a Strategy!

When I woke up this morning and looked at the clock, it was 3:56 a.m. I wondered if something would really, actually come by my house at 4:00 o'clock in the morning. The sheep had all been counted, and recounted and were all counted out, so at 3:59 a.m., I wandered out to the curb in front of my house and waited doubtfully for 4:00 a.m. to come and go. To my surprise, that vintage red and black biplane drifted silently down out of the night sky, sliding smoothly to the slickest three point landing that a French Poodle could ever make, then taxied to my curbside, while its giant radial engine sputtered and fell silent and its shiny polished spinner slowed to a stop.

I sauntered over to the pilot and asked, "Can you take me to Toy Land?" Without a word, the big black poodle hit the starter, the engine barked loudly then rattled to life. There is no talking after a big radial engine roars to life. We were air born in less than a hundred feet but instead of climbing up into the night sky, we kept gathering speed, barely clearing the treetops and telephone poles. We continued to accelerate as telephone poles zoomed by like picket fences, then blurred into the infinity of speed and time.

The engine began to cough intermittently, as the propeller slowed and we fell out of the sky into another time and into another place, 'Toy Land'. We touched down on the dry, dusty, dirt runway from my childhood where friends and I ventured, uninvited, to touch the delicate fabric skin and tails of a Piper Cub or a Stinson Voyager or sometimes an ancient biplane.

The old round top hangers were still there with the engineless yellow Cub still waiting for repair and the greasy crop duster waiting to take on another load of poison for the butterflies and the honeybees. I walked aimlessly around kicking dirt into open gopher holes which often snared the small rubber tire of an unwary pilot who strayed from the rutted dirt taxi way.

I found my old rusty, red, Radio Flyer wagon piled high with its memories of friends from my childhood but they are all gone now, lost to time and troubles. I picked up its faded black handle and trudged down the rutted dirt road towards the asphalt that began somewhere over the hill ahead. Somehow all of my friends had fallen victim to one deadly sin or another.

Kenny fell to the siren's call. Gordon smoked himself into the grave. Billy Joe lived to eat and died because of it. Randy was so proud, always so proud. Nothing mattered to him more than his pride. Charley made so much money, too much money, more than any man could ever spend but it was never enough, never enough. His X wives got it all in the end anyway. Evert killed a man out of plain meanness. He was always so angry. Nothing ever made him happy. He was just plain mad at the world. Jim Bo, well Jim Bo never changed.

When I finally made it to the pavement, I turned around and saw that everything had bounced out of my little red Radio Flyer wagon somewhere along the bumpy dirt road I had been traveling. The only thing that was still left in the little wagon was a small wooden trunk with its domed lid. I forced its rusty lock open, hoping that it might somehow be a time capsule, a relic from my past. Inside I found a small piece of crumpled paper. On it was penciled in large upper case letters:

HOPE ALWAYS DIES LAST!'

The Last Row

Philip, the magic horse, the Other and I had gone through the Door to Tomorrow. What we saw in the near future made me so sad that I was unable to go back to sleep. At 1:59 a.m. I went outside and waited for the Night Bus to come. It comes by here at 2:00 a.m. every morning. The bus arrived right on time. It came down the street towards me more slowly and quietly than usual, perhaps it was sensing my disappointment with the things awaiting all of us in the coming days. The bus stopped directly in front of me and Brad, the raccoon driver, opened the door with the swing of his lever. He sat there staring down at me, awaiting my personal request.

I said to Brad, "Take me somewhere into my future. Take me to my future as a writer, if one actually exists." Usually the journey begins and ends in seconds but this trip was different. We proceeded slowly, in the dark at first and then the moon came up, full and bright, as we passed trees and grass but no buildings or houses or cars or people, just landscapes. The Night Bus finally came to rest in a cul-de-sac in a beautiful park. Brad opened the door of the bus and waited. I descended down the steps of the bus into a giant cemetery with row after row of neat headstones, each with the name of a famous writer. As I passed each headstone, and I touched it, their stories sprang to life, Maya Angelo, Charles Dickens, John Steinbeck. There was Lenny alive again.

I turned around to go back to the bus but Brad motioned with his hand or paw, for me to proceed. Raccoons do have little hands you know that get them into all sorts of trouble. So I turned and continued down the neat rows of identical granite stones with dates and names from the past inscribed on them until I came to the very last row. There was an open hole in the green grass with a stone resting on its side, with my name spelled out across it, all in upper case letters and my date of birth was there on its upturned surface. Fortunately for me, there was no date of my departure chiseled yet into its polished granite face.

When I returned to the bus I asked Brad, the driver, what I should make of what I had just seen. He grinned and chuckled a raccoon chuckle through his pointy raccoon teeth but said nothing. Brad proceeded to drive me back home slowly, while I pondered this night's adventures. He stopped across the street in front of my house to let me off, for the bus was now headed in the opposite direction. After he left me, I stood there in the moonlight taking in this view of the house in which I live. It stood out from all of the others. There was that lush lawn of green, wood violets with the burbling fountain in its center, the huge olive tree, the three Apple Anna trees laden with tons of green fruit, the two lemon trees, the fig tree and the two giant Brazilian Mesquites, not to mention the Algerian Ivy, the loquats, the jujube and the winding brick paved pathway leading through the violets to the redwood doors which I had made myself. The first door was only half a door, to keep the dogs inside. The second door was made of heavy solid redwood planks, with bolted Z shaped cross bracing to keep strangers out.

    This old redbrick house stood there, so out of place, surrounded by its jungle of flowers and trees and plants of every kind and its fishponds and wishing well and swimming pool, its large pagoda, Jacuzzi and wandering brick pathways.

    This house and I seem so out of place, here in the middle of cactus and tumble weed country, in the middle of a dry, dry desert... here in the very last row.

12:59...Roger...Rabbit

The mind does many funny things, as you grow older. This morning, I woke up and stared at the large red numbers on the face of the digital clock. It read 12:58 a.m. I wondered what if anything, comes at 1:00 a.m. in the morning. I went out to the curb in front of our house at 12:59 and looked down its darkened street for any signs of movement. Before I knew it, a tricycle Harley came roaring around the corner and barreled down the street towards me. It screeched to a halt directly in front of me. I jumped on, still dressed in my red plaid flannel pajamas and we roared off on an adventure. The driver turned his head halfway around and shouted "Where to?" Instinctively I responded, "Take me to the moon!" In the blink of an eye, Roger Rabbit and I were roaring full speed around and around in circles on the surface of the moon kicking up billowing clouds of moon dust.

When I next awoke, it was 1:58 a.m. I wondered if anything could possibly come at 2:00 a.m. I trudged back out to the front of the house and waited. A vintage biplane, red and black, touched down at the end of the street, taxied to a stop at my driveway and I jumped into the front hole closest to the top wing. The engine roared to life and we sailed up and away, into the starlit night sky. The pilot kept squawking and banging on the side of the plane. I turned around. There at the controls was a big black, Poodle wearing goggles, a leather flight cap and a long scarf billowing back into the slipstream. We were circling around and around. The Poodle obviously wanted to know where I wanted to go.

"Peace of Mind" I shouted back to him. "Take me to that place, Peace of Mind." I drifted off to sleep staring up at the Big Dipper star formation in the night sky, mesmerized by the heat and droning exhaust sounds from the biplane's rattling, radial engine.

This reminded me of those summertime adventures with my older brother. We would ride all night, next to the droning gas-driven generator producing heat and illuminating the darkness for the huge Caterpillar earth-moving machine that my Father was driving around and around compacting the earth at night for the construction of the new runway at the airbase. We rode in back up on top of a huge pile of dirt, in the belly of the monstrous machine, falling asleep staring up into the night sky at the Big Dipper.

At 12: 59, my Father would park the monster at the end of the new runway, dim its glowing lights, silence the droning generator, and yell up at his two sleeping passengers, "Quitting Time!" and we would return to the world of the normal.

It is the custom at our house to say 'Rabbit' to each other when we wake up on the first day of each new month. Today is not the first day of the month but it is Mother's Day and it is also the first day of the rest of our life together.

I am getting up early and going out to the kitchen to mix up some batter for my Mother's favorite old fashion oatmeal cookies, made with lots of raisins, brown sugar, loads of really, real butter, and tons of love.

No matter how old you become, it's always a good day to make your mother her favorite cookies and to call and tell your mother that you love her, especially on 'Mother's Day.'

"ROGER...ROGER... I copy that. Every day should be "Mother's Day!"

An open letter to anyone who has a Mother

This morning, after I wrote this story for my mother and baked her favorite cookies for her, as a token of my love and appreciation for all of the many things she did for me and our family when I was growing up, I called her to wish her a Happy Mother's Day and to schedule a convenient time to deliver these home made cookies.

The phone rang and rang and rang. I thought that perhaps she was still at church. Finally, my older brother, Jim, answered her phone. He said that there were eight men there. They were paramedics and firemen. They were going to chopper my mother to TMC for emergency care. Jim said that her oxygen saturation had fallen to 72. She began to hallucinate and shake violently, claw at the empty air, so he had called 911. I asked my brother to keep me informed as to what was transpiring.

Choppers may be fast but they have to come from somewhere and they have to land someplace then they have to return to the hospital with their patient. Eventually my mother was transported to the emergency department at Tucson Medical Center. They stabilized her condition and treated her with dignity and respect. They admitted her and kept her in the hospital for two nights, before she was discharged.

I visited my mother the next day when she was stable and finally had her own room in the hospital and was no longer in a cubical or in the hallway of the emergency room. When I got to her room, my mother had just received a small bowl of broth from the nurse, which she ate slowly.

I gave her the story and told her that it was her Mother's Day gift that I had written for her. She held the typed story up to the light and slowly read it with her failing eyes. I watched her face as she wrinkled her brow, then slowly smiled. When she told me that she had never read anything like that before but she liked it, I saw that she had a tear in her eye. I gave her the oatmeal cookies I had made just the way she liked them.

She offered cookies to the male nurse but he graciously declined saying he was on a diet. She ate her cookie very slowly, smiling the whole time.

They had diagnosed my Mother's condition, on Mother's Day, as aerophagia. Aeorphagia literally translates as 'eating air'. She was alone at home on Mother's Day. No one had come to visit with her. She was doing what mothers have always done, to make something out of nothing, to create a meal out of thin air.

She wasn't alone on Mother's Day, she was in the E. R. surrounded by lots of caring people but they were not her family. They were not her children and they were not her grandchildren but they cared for her just the same.

I didn't get to see my mother on that Mother's Day and I didn't get to give her the gifts I had made for her. But, she understood, as mothers always do, when I gave her a big hug and reminded her that I love her and I always will.

Don't forget to give your Mother a big hug. Tell her that you love her and that you always will. You never know when goodbye will be farewell.

Making Smoke

This morning, while I was contemplating whether I should get up yet or continue to drag my feet about it, this apparition appeared above me. I recognized this character from a past encounter many years ago. "Aren't you that smoke guy," I asked? He said that he was the Smoke Chief. He was Native American, dressed from head to toe in buckskin, wearing a full feather headdress. I asked why he was there. He said that he had come to show me how to 'make smoke.'

He took a pinch of dried, shredded tobacco, dipped his fingers in water and formed the tobacco into little cones. After making several of these small cones he went back to the first one and began modifying the cones by forcing his thumb into their base, leaving a small indentation. "Let these cones dry before you light them," he said. Next he took a flattened piece of what he said was the inside core from a cactus plant. It was about the size and shape of a stick of butter, sliced in half longwise and then lain side by side. He began wrapping a strip of cactus fiber around and around the cactus core. He started winding in the center and moved toward its base, then back to the center and up towards its top. The end result resembled a small bowling pin about six inches tall with its bottom quarter cut off.

He said to use these as a base upon which to place the tobacco cones, before you lite them with the burning end of a dried reed. He illustrated this process by setting up several of these units around a sick person, who was lying on a pallet on the ground. He said that the smoke could be used to see what was wrong with a sick person or to see into the future. I asked if it was all right to use store bought tobacco. He said, "No way. You have to use wild tobacco, or grow your own from seed, then air dry them and shred them or shred them while they're still green and then dry the leaves."

He said that he would return to show me how to use smoke to 'see into the future.' Then he vanished.

I thought about this for a while. I came to the conclusion that the Smoke Chief had come because I had been working on getting the basics down on how to use 'The Event Horizon' to see future events before they happen for almost a week now but with only modest success.

Red Face, Red Man

This morning, late, about 4:30 a.m., I saw an eye, from a side angle perspective. Eyes are almost always portals to something or somewhere. I never pass up an opportunity to see what lies behind an eye, no matter how tired I am.

I entered the eye and there in front of me was a red face. Not devil red and not barn red but a really tanned red, like only a real purebred Plains Indian could possibly have. His skin appeared to be really weathered. His face had sunken cheeks, free of any surplus fat. His salt and pepper gray hair was bound around with a leather strap. A couple of feathers and various other curiosities adorned his thick locks that trailed down behind his back. His deerskin attire was as weathered as the thin skin on his hands. They moved deftly. His right hand held a hand carved wooden spoon, while his left hand held an elongated dried gourd bowl. He put a spoonful of refried pinto beans into the bowl, then a couple of spoons full of boiled white rice, followed by two slices of yellow squash and finally the end of a green onion with all of its roots intact, which had been boiled until it was completely cooked.

After the bowl was filled, the Red Man turned and kneeled down next to the same infirmed man that was on the pallet, on the floor, in 'Making Smoke' He then stuffed all of the food into the sick man's mouth and forced him to eat all of it. Then he started hitting the sick man on his chest with the same wooden spoon which he just finished using to stuff the food into the man's mouth.

A hole opened up in the man's chest and out flew what looked like a black bat with a long lizard-like tail. Closely behind this bat like creature, came pairs of brown clumps of something. Pair after pair of these clumps trailed away after the bat-like creature, as it disappeared into the sky. After nine or ten of these pairs had left the man's chest and vanished, the opening in the man's chest closed leaving no sign that it had been there. The comatose man opened his eyes and looked around.

The entire scene vanished in the blink of an eye. I was again in my own bed staring up at a blank ceiling.

Wararies

Wednesday night I went to visit Dream Walker. I had not seen him for quite awhile. So, I journeyed to the gateway to his world. I sat down to wait for him to come because he always came in short order but he never showed up. I became quite concerned for his safety, so I entered through the gateway marked by the two large poles and began looking for him. I was very familiar with his world. He gave me the gift of dream walking. He taught me how to dream walk and he showed me all of the rituals that went with its practice. I investigated his wigwam, his fire pit, his sacred places but he was nowhere to be found. I sensed that he was near his sacred mountain that was actually a very large hill. There on the backside was the entrance to a cave that had not been present before. It was very dark and spooky inside.

The entrance to this lair was narrow and just tall enough for me to enter without ducking my head. I pulled out the glowing disc that I carry with me on a leather string around my neck. The light emitted from this disc is similar to the light from a full moon. For some reason, the light was being absorbed before it reached the walls of the cave. For additional lighting, I drew the glowing sword with its shimmering reflective surfaces. It too failed to illuminate the cave walls. But, sets of yellow eyes could be seen reflected from the polished surface of the sword. As I moved deeper into the cave it widened into a large central arena where a single wooden pole protruded straight up out of the ground. Tied to the pole with heavy rope slumped the Dream Walker.

I approached the Dream Walker with caution, leaned down and whispered into his ear, "I'm going to cut you loose. Follow me out of here." There was no response. Next, I administered a secret potion that reverses the effects of any toxin. Again, there was no reaction. That's when I knew I would have to carry him out on my shoulder. I deftly cut the heavy ropes with the magical half sword and hoisted Dream Walker onto my shoulder. With the glowing disc dangling from the leather string around my neck and with my shimmering sword held tightly in my right hand, I turned around to make my way back out of the cave. Then I saw them. There were several of them blocking my path. They looked like skinny, black, giant gingerbread men with glowing yellow eyes. They had no noses and no buttons or any other decorations, just three lips and two round yellow eyes. With slashing sword and swaying disc, we made for the entrance to the cave.

By the time I saw the light of day, I was panting heavily. They failed to follow us as we made for Dream Walker's home. I put his limp body down on the thin sleeping mat on the floor in the center of his wigwam. I was at a complete loss. I had no idea what to do for Dream Walker but I knew that he wouldn't make it unless something was done for him. I had to leave. I had to get help.

My first thought was to go to the Wizard. He was in Ireland restoring the Glen and its river ways, so the leprechauns could return again to Ireland. I found him near the tree where he sleeps at night. He told me that he couldn't leave now because his work was at a critical juncture but he advised me to go back to Never Land and ask the leprechauns for their assistance. "They will know what to do," he said. So, back I went to Never Land. I asked Jenkins what could be done for Dream Walker. He said, "Use all seven of the magic mosses to make a concoction, then force him to swallow it. Chop up all of the mosses very finely, add enough warm water to make a soupy mixture, then spoon it all down Dream Walker's throat." Jenkins gathered the mosses, chopped them very finely and prepared them for me.

He handed me a flask of fresh stream water from the magical stream there in Never Land. "Hurry," he told me, "Time is of the essence."

I forced the green goop down Dream Walker's throat. He stirred a little, then awoke and began to share what had happened. He told me that that these creatures were Wararies and they were tearing apart his dream world. Wararies cook up and consume dreamscapes. I knew then that we needed a lot more than moss to get rid of these bandits. I told Dream Walker to stay away from the Wararies, while I was away finding some way to get rid of them. "I'll be back!" I said. Then I left. I knew too that Dream Walker had depleted all of his energy in the futile effort to sustain his dream world and protect it from these marauders.

I went straight to the Source because this is where the endless supply of energy is located. Last month on the full moon, I received the gift of a magical pearl. It is about the size of a blueberry and has the power to store unlimited amounts of water. I wondered if it might also be able to store energy or light as well. Where the Source resides, there is brilliant white illumination. I removed the magic pearl from its secret pouch and exposed it to the unlimited light and the unlimited energy. Next I exposed the Other to the same forces, then together, the magical pearl, the Other and I, went back to the Dream Walkers Realm.

The Other is a luminous double of a sorcerer, which is indestructible and extremely powerful. It cannot be injured and cannot be killed. It is an extension of the sorcerer's will. I am not only a dream walker but also a powerful sorcerer who has created his own double, known as the Other.

The Other entered the cave of the Wararies. There was a brilliant flash of light and the Wararies came flying out of the cave, never to be seen again. I placed the magical pearl on top of the wooden pole in the large chamber of the cave, which the Wararies had made. The cave was illuminated in brilliant white light and an unending stream of water from the magical pearl began to flow. Dream Walker recovered immediately and began moving his personal belongings from his chilly wigwam into the warm cave with its bright light and endless stream of pure spring water.

The Spirit in the Pot

The Spirit in the Pot told me it needed to be in a dark, protected space in some kind of container for it to feel safe. So, I put it in one of the large ceramic Fu dogs which we have protecting the entrance to our house. My wife was not happy about having any more spirits around our house, even if the spirit were kept in the front yard. She wanted me to get rid of the spirit and for sure, to leave that ancient burial pot alone where it was abandoned in the alley.

I went out to catch the Night Bus that would be coming by at 2:00 o'clock in the morning and asked the Spirit if it would like to go along with me. It said,

"Definitely not!" So, I went out to the curb and waited for the bus to come. When the bus stopped and the driver opened the door, I asked the driver if he could take the Spirit in the Pot somewhere safe and help me to get rid of it. He looked puzzled, scratched his head with his raccoon fingers, gave it some thought and shook his head affirmatively up and down slowly.

I ran back to the Fu dog and grabbed the spirit. We jumped onto the bus and the driver started moving slowly down the street. He took a ninety-degree turn to the left which he had never done before. Then we entered a large tunnel. There were florescent lights strung intermittently along the ceiling in three rows. We kept gaining speed until the lights appeared to be a continuous blur, then the whole ceiling appeared to be completely illuminated. When we finally stopped and departed the bus, everything was just light, as though there were fog being illuminated from every direction, as though the fog itself was emitting light.

As we departed the bus the Spirit was transformed into a beautiful Indian maiden. She was dressed entirely in deerskin. Her dark hair was tightly braided in two long braids. The ends were wound tightly with strings of tiny beads of many colors for about one and one half inches near the very ends of the braids. Each braid was also secured at its base above her ears where the braids began by a wrapping of colored fibers. These appeared to be made of wool or bison hair spun or twisted into yarn. Her moccasins were very high and covered her lower legs completely. They had one large silver button on the outside of each moccasin. The upper portions of her moccasins were laced together with leather strips. Her skirt was long, well below the knee. Her long sleeve jacket came below her waist. It had decorative fringe several inches long down the back of each arm. There were several ceremonial silver bangles hanging from long leather strips adorning her jacket. She must have been the daughter of some high-ranking member of her tribe. My guess would be that she probably came from one of the plains tribes or possibly from Oklahoma. She was a very pretty young lady.

The Indian princess said that a powerful medicine man had imprisoned her spirit in the large pot and buried it in a cave. She didn't know what happened to her body and she had no idea how long she had been in the burial pot. My guess and that is only a guess, would be that she had been there for a couple of hundred years. She had no knowledge of the white man. She was so thankful to me for liberating her and bringing her here to the 'confluence of lights'. She came over to where I was sitting and kissed me on the forehead. Then this beautiful Indian Princess disappeared into the fog of light.

Indian in a Pot

City refuse collection is twice each year in our neighborhood. They pick up any unwanted items left in the alley. It seemed inappropriate for me to allow that large discarded, historic Indian Pot to be squashed and taken away to the City Dump, just because it was cracked. The fact that the pot contained the spirit of an Indian Princess for so many years just added to my dilemma. My wife didn't want me to bring the pot home. I didn't think it should be left in the alley, so I took it to the office for safe keeping, until I could find a home for it. One of the girls at the office placed a purple rosary in the pot, with most of the beads hanging out over its edge. Another of the girls at the office said that she had heard loud noises when she was there alone. It sounded like someone had entered the premises and was rummaging around in back but no one was there when she went to investigate.

I needed to get to the bottom of this situation with the 'Indian in the Pot'. I went in search of the Indian Princess who had come from the pot in question and disappeared into the fog of light. I eventually found her hiding in a deciduous forest. She was all dirty. Her deerskin clothing was badly torn and she had lost both of her moccasins.

I took her down to the river to bathe, while I got rid of the ragged clothing she had been wearing. She seemed to trust me completely, perhaps because I had already rescued her once from the pot in which she was imprisoned. When she came out of the river, I clothed her in a floor-length white silk dress, with a long, white silk scarf covering her dark waist-length braided hair.

Out of the forest burst this very muscular Indian warrior wearing buckskin trousers. His chest was bare. His head was partially shaven, with a long dark braid of hair protruding from the right side of his head above and behind his ear. He had a gold or copper band around his left bicep and a leather band tied with a thong around his right bicep. On his forehead he wore what looked like a red sweat band made of some kind of material tied in back of his head in a double knot. His face was twisted and angry. He cried out in a loud voice, "She is mine." He drew a large knife from beneath the leather belt around his waist as he moved towards me. He was way bigger than I am.

I summoned Raymond, the magic horse. He instantly materialized out of thin air. The Indian stopped in his tracks, frozen as though he had never even seen a horse before. This magnificent specimen is truly a huge horse, standing twenty hands at the shoulder and very muscular. I swept the Indian Princess up and onto the bare back of the horse, placing her sidesaddle, clinging to its long main. The Indian cried out again, "She belongs to me, Many Wolves."

Never tell a sorcerer your name. I summoned a pack of six wolves that immediately began circling around the Indian Warrior with their teeth bared, growling in unison, staring him down. Raymond, the magic horse, the Indian Princess and I transported to where her family lived, leaving the angry Indian Warrior encircled by six hungry wolves. Her father approached with great excitement upon seeing his beautiful daughter. The only thing he said to me was, "Many Moons!" I don't know if his name was Many Moons or her name was Many

Moons or if it had been many moons since he had last seen his daughter. I left them united in eternity and my office and the pot free of all spirits. It's all in a day's work for a sorcerer like me.

Long Bow

Last night, or more correctly, this morning at 1:00 o'clock, I went out to the street to catch a ride with Maurice, in his red & black biplane. I heard a plane coming in the distance but it didn't sound like the old biplane's engine. The sound tapered off quickly and was barely audible. Whatever kind of plane that was coming was lined up for a direct approach, with its engine throttled way down. It had landing lights, so I knew for sure, that it wasn't the old biplane. It touched down at the end of our street. The engines were shut down completely, as soon as the wheels touched the ground. I knew immediately that it was a C-47 or DC-3. It stopped directly in front of me. I went around to the other side of the plane and climbed up the ladder into the fuselage. It was a DC-3, but there were no seats in the bay area, so it must be used for hauling cargo. It was completely empty at the moment. I made my way up to the cockpit and sat down in the right seat. The captain was sitting in the left seat. He looked very familiar, even with his flight cap pulled down low on his forehead, his earphones covering his ears, and his aviator sunglasses covering his eyes, though it was quite dark outside. His thin dark mustache and chiseled features gave away his identity. This was Howard Hughes, in his prime. He turned and faced me but didn't say a word.

I told him I wanted to go someplace I needed to go to. I told him I needed to see something I needed to see. I told him I needed to know something I needed to know. He stared at me for a moment, then, he barked, "Grab the yoke. Push the throttle quadrant all the way forward. Move the yoke forward when the airspeed hits 40 knots. As soon as the tail comes up pull back on the yoke give it a little left rudder and keep the nose five degrees above the horizon. Straight out departure until airspeed reaches 170 knots. Make a shallow turn to port, until we reach 5 degrees magnetic heading. Climb to flight level 115. Pull back on the throttle quadrant and keep the RPM's at 1800. Watch the cylinder head temperatures. Don't run the engines too lean. Turn on the oxygen if you get light-headed. Maintain our airspeed between 175 and 180 knots, straight on till morning. I'll be asleep. Don't bother me unless there is an emergency."

As dawn broke to the east, I could see foothills and mountains in the distance. The captain began to stir as the darkness of night receded. He scanned the horizon, pointed at an expanse of grassland to the right of the foothills and said, "Good job. I'm going to put her down right there at the base of that mountain."

We were greeted by a friendly band of Indians. They had never seen an airplane before, so they treated us as royalty and invited us to join them in celebration and dance around their communal fire pit that evening. As the festivities waned, the chief introduced himself to us as Long Bow. He also introduced his wife and all of the elders. When he asked if we would smoke the ritual tribal peace pipe as a sign of friendship, I produced the peace pipe that was given to me by the father of the Indian Princess, I rescued from the pot. Long Bow exclaimed in great excitement, "This magnificent peace pipe you have could have only been made by someone from our tribe!" Then I filled the bowl of my peace pipe with the tribe's own tobacco and began to puff it, the smoke became a full size likeness of the beautiful Indian Princess. Long Bow sprang to his feet and cried out, "She is my Grandmother Many Moons!" Howard Hughes had brought us to the Black Hills of South Dakota. This was her tribe. This is where the pot belongs.

Heart of Gold

I was visiting my son in Orange County over the weekend. He was getting the pool house ready for expanded use. He asked me if I wanted to stay in the pool house or to stay in the main house in the guest room. I chose to stay in the pool house so I could check it out and make suggestions about what was still needed to make it more functional.

We were also upgrading the pool lighting so it was late when I retired for the evening. Before I went to sleep I checked the place out. There was an Inca warrior standing in the corner of the room by the front door. He was wearing robust looking sandals and a short skirt of some kind. In his left hand he held a short spear upright with its bottom resting on the floor. It was about five feet long. In his right hand he held a small shield about eleven inches wide and twenty inches tall. It was rectangular in shape and was oriented vertically like the spear. On his left wrist he wore a leather bracelet about seven inches wide. He also wore a headband that was ornately decorated with geometric patterns. It was about an inch and one quarter wide and was woven from some kind of white colored plant fibers. On his left arm and shoulder were intricate tattoos. His face had lines tattooed on it. His eyes and the bridge of his nose were also tattooed raccoon-like with an ornate filigreed pattern. I tried to communicate with him several times but he just stood there like a statue not moving a muscle and not responding to my inquiries.

 I went out onto the deck near the pool and there stood this Inca Princess with long dark hair clothed in a floor length white robe made of some lite-weight white material. She had been swimming in the pool. I asked her what she was doing there. We were able to communicate but with difficulty. She told me that the Inca warrior was her official personal protector. He traveled everywhere with her. It took some effort but she was finally able to communicate to me that she had been chosen as an Inca princess at an early age and was destined to be sacrificed to the Gods. She had to be a pristine virgin at the time of her sacrifice. The warrior was given the task of protecting her at all times and preserving her purity for the sacrificial offering. She had found her way to me to help her recover her heart that had been ripped out of her chest and offered to the Gods while it was still beating.

The princess then showed me where her heart was located in a vision. It was at the center of some kind of complex matrix where it was still beating keeping the matrix it was connected to functioning. When I told her that I found her entire story to be difficult to believe, she opened her robe revealing a giant hole in her chest where her heart had been ripped out of her body. I told her that I had no idea how I could possible accomplish such a crazy task.

She took my hand and placed it into the hole in her chest and we were all instantly transported back to the time and place where the sacrificial offering was transpiring. The princess was tied on the sacrificial stone. The high priest was standing over her with his flint dagger raised high in the air. His face grimaced. His eyes squinted out from behind raccoon-like tattoos as the sun broke above the distant horizon. I opened the lid of the small domed box and time stood still. I jerked the sacrificial stone dagger from his clinched fists and plunged it deep into his chest cracking several ribs free from their attachments to his sternum. I ripped his beating heart out and placed it into his grasping hands held high above his head. Then, I closed the domed lid of the small box and time resumed. His own heart became the sacrifice to the Gods.

Her personal protector sliced the leather straps restraining the princess and the three of us escaped back into the future as the high priest collapsed still clinging to his own beating heart. My hand was now held against the smooth unblemished skin of the Inca princess' chest. She smiled at me and said, "We traveled all this way to find you because we were told that you were a great sorcerer and could save me from the dreadful death that awaited me. Thank you so much. My protector and I can now share our lives together." They turned and disappeared together into a dense jungle setting somewhere in their past. I was left standing alone in front of the pool house at my son's house in Orange County, contemplating what had just transpired.

Itsacono

Sharing this experience is intended only to expand the arena of possibility for you. I was awake and in bed when images about six inches square began to appear in my field of vision. These images were the same with my eyes open or with them closed. An image would form then some parts of it would animate and then that image would be replaced by another image emerging from the right side of my field of vision and exiting to the left side of my field of vision. It was almost like a slide show. This process continued for a long time. I was trying to figure out how this process was possible. The images appeared to be elaborate etchings or engravings to be used to illustrate books or papers from a long time ago before there were any photographs available. The content appeared to be from the fourteenth or fifteenth century based on the subjects and the subject matter. I don't know what they were supposed to refer to. While focused on this process a scene from a dense jungle momentarily appeared. Between the leaves I saw part of a face staring out at me. It was the left eye and cheek of a person. I noticed the glint in the eye as well as the white sclera when the eye moved. It appeared to me to be the face of an Inca Indian. Their faces are unique. I didn't know for sure if it were the face of a female or of a younger male but I was determined to find that person.

It took a while but I located him in the jungle deep in the past. I presented myself in a small clearing in the jungle as an Aborigine dressed only in a leather thong given to me by Aru the keeper of Dream Time. As he circled around me I moved to face him as though I were standing on a turntable. Communication was clear and precise though neither he nor I moved our lips. Communication must have been telepathic. He told me that his mother's dying wish was for him to find the Sorcerer who had rescued her and his warrior father from certain death.

I asked if she were still alive. He said that she was. He took me to her. She was lying in her bed waiting for death to take her. She had cataracts and was blind. I magically removed her cataracts and she could see once again but she didn't recognize me in my present form as an Aborigine. I told her that I was a shape-shifter and transformed myself back into a familiar form. Because she could now see once again she resumed her daily activities and I departed back into my own time.

I asked the Source how that whole process could have transpired and how the Inca Prince could have located me far in the future. He said that we must share some history. We must have some connection. I wondered if he possibly could have been a prior incarnation of myself. To test this hypothesis I went to the edge of the abyss and crossed over on the 'Wizard's Bridge'. On the other side of the abyss standing on the right side of that end of the bridge are all of my former incarnations. The Inca Prince was there among them. He was a former incarnation of myself. The Source told me some time ago that I must locate each of my past and future incarnations and meld with them before I would be complete. I put the Inca Prince on like you would put on a Hawaiian shirt and then went through the 'Door of No Return' and we were one. I had gone back in time and saved the Inca Princess and her warrior guard who became the parents of the Inca Prince who summoned me from the future at his mother's request. Itsacono the Inca prince was a prior incarnation of myself.

The State of Affairs

Periodically, my wife asks me to give her the state of affairs. This means she wants an assessment of the current mental state of each member of our extended family.

I gathered information for everyone including my wife. Normally I go out of my way to exclude myself from this process because I believe ignorance is truly bliss. However, apparently my mind wandered a bit and some things must have leaked through.

This really, really, ugly, fat face of an Indian, with a cauliflower nose, worse than W.C. Fields appeared. Then the side view of the bust of another, smaller Indian man, appeared on the left. He held up the closed fist of his left hand and allowed some kind of dust to trickle out as he blew air from his mouth. Out of the dust appeared a very small Indian Princess the size of a Barbie Doll. Then everything disappeared. I had no idea what that was about.

I got up a little after 3:00 o'clock in the morning and went to the bathroom. When I returned, I was wide awake, so I decided to check with the Dream Walker to see if he could provide me with any information about the images of the three Indians I had seen earlier.

I entered the dreamscape, went to the gateway of Dream Walker's dream world and waited for him to arrive. He usually comes quickly when anyone approaches the gateway to his world. After waiting a few minutes, I sat down with my legs crossed as though I were going to meditate. He failed to arrive, so I decided to enter his world even though that is considered to be quite rude.

The closest place in his world, where I thought he might be, was at his fire pit where he performed his spiritual rituals. He wasn't there. I again sat down on the ground with legs crossed as though I would meditate and waited. Again, he failed to show up. This was very unusual for him. I was concerned for his well being and continued next to his mud home where he was once again not to be found. I repeated the process of sitting down crossed my legs and waited but nothing happened. Next I went to the cave where Dream Walker had taken up residence when I was here the last time. He wasn't there either. The last place where he might be was on top of the mountain (which was actually a large hill) where he gave thanks to the four cardinal directions.

The hilltop was deserted. I sat down in the center of the hill where Dream Walker would sit. I summoned the four winds. As the winds whirled around me, the old Indian Man appeared, raised his hand, releasing ashes. From the ashes emerged the full-sized Indian Princess. "Who are you?" I asked. "She Walker" was her reply. She came to me extending her right hand saying, "Take my hand. Do not let go."

I took her hand. We walked through a shimmering curtain into paradise. I looked all around, took out my sword and looked into its reflection. There was nothing.

None of this was real. I put the sword away. In front of us was a pond with the shape of a perfect circle. It was filled with billowing fog with radiant light coming from its depths. She led me to its edge and we jumped in.

I landed on solid ground with smoke all around. In the center was Dream Walker tied to a burning stake. I rushed towards him, slashed the leather thongs and we were standing alone in the open air on top of the hill. I asked him what was going on? Dream Walker told me that the princess was 'She Walker,' that the old Indian was a seer, that the ugly Indian was a 'Dream Demon.' He said that he had summoned the four winds and ended up falling into the 'Dream Demons' trap, like an ant into the ant lion's lair and that the fire around the pole where he was tied was consuming all of his memories and his memories were all that he was.

Dream Walker thanked me and told me that I had mastered the art of dreaming, that I was in a dream, within a dream, within a dream.

I told Dream Walker that I was completely awake the whole time. He put his hand on my shoulder and said that only a 'master dreamer' could have saved him from certain annihilation.

De – Termination

I visited with the Facilitator and Sabatini last evening. They were sitting on the park bench facing west with the sandy beach before them and the ocean of the event horizon stretching out into the distance as far as the eye could see. They had made a habit of sitting there for some time now. I asked them if there were some reason for them to be always sitting on that park bench, there in front of the event horizon, facing west. "Why not sit in some other place or in some other direction?" I asked. They both retorted together in unison, "What do you think?"

I told them that I believed that there must be something in that direction, in the future, that they wanted me to engage. They both agreed that was indeed why they had been sitting there for months now. They both think that I am rather slow on the draw and a little dim-witted. I told them that I wasn't sure that I would be able to do all of the things required with such an undertaking. They said for me to just try.

The first step in the process was to get a little help for this unknown project. The Facilitator said he was not going to be going out there into the open ocean. Sabatini agreed to go along for this excursion into the unknown. In the end, Sabatini, the Traveler's Buddha and Lucky, the child, accompanied me on this odyssey. The first challenge was to calm the ocean. The second challenge was to locate the event that I was looking for. It was worse than looking for the proverbial needle in a haystack. The ocean is a really big place. The next step involved solidifying the surface of the waters and stopping the movement of time. The last step involved intervention in the upcoming future event.

This event was the impending termination of an important player on the national scene, in the near future. The open coffin was already prepared for the demise of this person. That person was already in place in the coffin but the lid was yet to be closed. The deal was yet to be consummated. My task was to intervene at the most opportune moment and prevent this event from actually becoming a reality. In these activities, like many things that happen in life, timing is everything.

There was no room in this process for any of my own personal feelings, beliefs, biases, or preferences to play any role. My task was to prevent this particular person from dying, at this particular moment in time.

I did that. The child remained on the surface of the ocean and provided for us an anchor in a definite place in a definite time, in a definite space and in a definite reality. Sabatini held fast to the child's hand, with one hand and he held tight to my hand with his other hand, thus allowing me to be able to function effectively in a specific time in the future. Sabatini told me later that I would not have survived the trip through the various realities without his assistance.

Once again I had chosen wisely and correctly those who accompanied me and assisted me on this perilous adventure.

The Source later told me that he definitely would not have put any money on my chances of actually pulling off this rescue, by traveling into the future. None-the-less, he was quite impressed with my success and with my de–termination of this important person in the future, by utilizing the event horizon.

Adept's School of Knowledge

I woke up early Saturday morning and found myself wearing a black cotton robe with its hood hanging down on my back and long black pajama-like pants. My head was shaved and I was wearing sandals. I looked up and saw a lot of adult males similarly dressed all coming from different directions headed towards this large square brick building five stories high in front of us. On the face of the building up near its top, in large letters, was the name, "Adept School of Knowledge".

Last night, I was working in the third attention, the place of emptiness, when the Source suggested that I revisit the Adept School of Knowledge, so I opened a portal and transported over there. No one was around. I entered through the double doors. The door on the right side opened inward and the door on the left side opened outward. Inside there was a long hallway about two meters wide and more than a hundred meters in length. There were no doorways, nor were there any light fixtures or switches anywhere, yet there was an even level of illumination. The walls, the floor and the ceiling were all a uniform light-gray color. I walked the entire length of the hall. It ended in a 'T' shaped intersection with an identical hallway at right angles going to the left and to the right. I turned left and went down that hallway. It was the same as the one I had just traversed, with no doors, light fixtures or switches and a uniform level of illumination. I followed it to its end where it turned ninety degrees to the left. At the end of each hall there was another left turn. This continued as each hall became shorter, like a maze in a cornfield, until it finally ended in a square room a little more than two meters in dimension. The entrance disappeared creating a square space.

In the center of the room was a square pillow on the floor, with a Chinese -style ladies' folding hand fan on top of it. It was a pillow like the ones people use to sit on when they meditate. Instead of picking up the fan and sitting down on the pillow, I took out my rose-colored glasses which allows me to see things as they are instead of how they appear to be and the fan now appeared to be a tall white wading bird, like a crane. The pillow became a big pile of bird droppings.

Next I took out the double-lensed, magical pince-nez spectacles that show things as they really are and the bird droppings turned into a pile of gold coins, while the white bird became a creature comprised of pure energy. Then, I took out the 'sword of truth' whose reflection shows the true nature of something, and the pile of gold coins were replaced with a bottomless black hole and the creature made of energy turned into a wisp of spiraling smoke. I swung the sword with great force striking the cloud of smoke. Everything instantly disappeared. I was alone in the room with the pillow and the fan. The room was oriented with each corner pointing in a cardinal direction. I re-oriented the pillow and sat down facing west. I positioned the fan pointing north, meditated, and entered the place of emptiness where only the Source exists. I heard a humming sound…mmm, that grew and became a defining AHHH… It was the sound of a thousand meditating monks chanting their mantras. I became the sound itself.

The Source said to me, "I see that you have just had your first lesson at the Adept School of Knowledge." I asked the Source, "What was the lesson and what was I supposed to have learned from that whole experience." The source said to me, "The first and most important lesson is, 'Nothing is what it appears to be'…ever!"

Hidden Arena

The next night, I returned to the Adept School of Knowledge. There were seven steps up to its entrance. I wasn't positive that I counted seven steps correctly, so I went back down the steps and recounted them again for a third time as I climbed back up the steps. When I was focused on recounting them for the third time, I noticed a silver toe ring on the big toe of my left foot. I have never had a toe ring on any of my toes before. I opened the double doors expecting to once again find that long hallway but instead, there was this huge open arena with row after row of terraced spaces where seats could have been and probably should have been but they were completely devoid of any seating, as though designed for standing or for an audience of sitting meditators. I started down the steps, moving towards the central stage of this giant amphitheater. When I reached the last step at the bottom, I had counted to a total of seventy-two terraces. That is a lot of steps and a lot of terraces

When I stepped out onto the central stage, it instantly became a wide, open meadow, complete with thick, lush, green, green grass. In the distance were hedgerows of verdant trees. As I took in the panoramic view, the arena itself had disappeared and was now a continuation of this expansive green meadow. I walked into the grassy field and lay down in its lush soft grass. I sank into the grass and became the grass. I sank into the moist soil and became the soil. A small plant sprouted and grew up out of the soil, and I became that plant. It was a sunflower. It bloomed and I became the large yellow sunflower. A beautiful butterfly landed on the flower and I became the butterfly. The butterfly fluttered away and joined hundreds of other butterflies and I became the migration of butterflies. The butterflies became twinkling stars in the night sky and I became the twinkling stars.

I returned to the third attention and asked the Source what the whole experience was all about. The Source said, "That was the second lesson from the Adept School of Knowledge. The seventy-two steps represent the seventy-two years you have spent in this life's experience. The process of lying down in the green meadow embodies your death and assimilation into the grass itself and into the soil and into the flowers and into the insects and eventually completing the circle of life and its ultimate connection to the stars themselves. This then is the lesson of impermanence, nothing is permanent, every thing changes. There are no exceptions to the rule of impermanence."

The next night I returned again to The Adept School of Knowledge. This time I checked on the side of the building before I went inside. The building was a mere façade. It was only one brick in thickness. When I climbed the seven steps up to the entrance, I noticed a second silver toe ring on the second toe of my left foot symbolizing that I had been given the second lesson from the Adept School of Knowledge. I entered the School of Knowledge through the double doors and there was only darkness. There was absolutely nothing there, no light, no walls, no ceiling, no floor, no sound, and no movement. There was only emptiness. Out of the emptiness emerged a splotchy glowing orb. Then, a second orb materialized. The Source said that the first orb was our universe; the second orb was a parallel universe. They merged and became one. The emptiness filled with countless other universes and the Source said, "This is the fourth attention. It is the workshop of God. Here exist an infinite number of universes."

Into the Light

The next night I returned to the Adept School of Knowledge, and once again there was an additional silver ring on the next toe of my left foot signifying yet another lesson hopefully learned. The first lesson was that, "Nothing is what it appears to be, ever!"

The second lesson was that, "Nothing is permanent, everything changes!"

The third lesson was that, "The fourth attention exists and it is the workshop of God where there exists an infinite number of universes!"

When I opened the door to the School of Knowledge this time there was pure white light. I walked into the light. Everything was light. Everything was made up of light, even the floor itself. As I proceeded further into the light a familiar figure emerged from within the white mist of light. I first met him several years ago while I was time traveling in his location and in his time period. I spent quite a bit of time walking along with him and talking with him as he journeyed through the countryside. He was dark complexioned, had long dark brown hair and a short scruffy beard. His nose was maybe one size too large for his face. He was about five feet eight inches tall. His clothing was rather shabby. His name was Jesus. I greeted him in his traditional manner with a hug.

Next, out of that dense white mist emerged another person whom I had met for the first time last year. He was shorter and chubbier, about five feet five inches tall. His name was Abraham. Then a shorter man still, whom I had never met before emerged. He introduced himself as Mohammed. I asked him if he were the Prophet Mohammed. He said that he was. I had never seen a picture of the Prophet Mohammed, so I had no idea what he actually looked like. I had always assumed that he was larger and physically more imposing than he turned out to be.

They each told me that this is where true believers came when they died. They came into the light and were greeted by Jesus or by Abraham or by Mohammed, depending on their personal faith and from there they would make their way to where they would begin their new existence. I of course had to ask the next most logical question for me. What about the Hindu and the Buddhist believers? Out of the mist emerged Krishna, whom I had first encountered many years ago when we were visiting in India. So it seems, that each believer is met in their after life by that individual who most personifies their belief system.

I then asked two more questions. One, "how does the assignment process unfold?" and two, "what happens to the non-believers?" They told me that each person self-assigns their destiny by turning away from the light when they encounter whatever attracts their attention as they walk past different events and situations that are constantly unfolding on either side of the path.

Non-believers shun the light and turn away, seeking the comfort and familiarity from their own darkness. Later, I checked with a Buddha that I have known for several years regarding who greets them when they arrive. The Buddha said, "They are greeted by themselves. For those who follow the path of the Buddha seek enlightenment through their own efforts with the aid of the Dharma."

Illusion

This was the day of the full moon for November. I awoke at 12:23 a.m. and checked for crows outside. There was one small, magical crow about two and a half feet tall on the lowest wire in the alley behind my house. That would make it the telephone or cable wire not the power lines.

I went outside and sat down on the brick pavers near the pool. The single crow flew down and landed directly in front of me. This crow was the smallest of any magical crow that I have encountered thus far. It came very close to me and sat down and just stared at me. I tried to communicate with it but it just continued to stare at me. After awhile, I started to close my eyes and drift off. Each time this happened, the crow would come closer and begin pecking on my left shoulder until I woke up. Then it would sit back down and continue to stare at me. After about an hour and a half of this pecking routine each time my attention drifted, it was getting close to 2:00 o'clock, when the Night Bus would come by, so I asked the small magical crow if it wanted to accompany me on the night bus. The crow nodded its head in the affirmative, so we wandered through the house and on out under the street light to await the arrival of the bus that would be coming in a couple of minutes.

When the bus arrived and the folding door opened, I told the crow to tell the bus driver where it wanted to go. The magical crow perched on the handrail just behind the driver and whispered in his ear the desired destination then we were off on an unknown adventure. I never heard where we were going but I must have fallen asleep during the process because the next thing I remember was waking up in my back yard with the crow sitting directly in front of me with its head tucked under its left wing apparently asleep.

After a couple of hours more of this sleeping crow with its head under its left wing, I decided to check it out with the rose-colored glasses to see if it actually was a crow or if it were something else. With the rose-colored glasses, it remained a crow. With the double-lensed pince-nez spectacles it still remained a crow but with the reflection from the magical Sword of Truth, it became a skeleton of a crow.

I picked the crow up and it seemed to be stiff and cold like a stuffed animal. I didn't know what to do with it. I tried several things but nothing seemed to be working. I couldn't leave it in the yard but I didn't want to take it into Never Land because I didn't know what it was. I thought it might be a 'Trojan Crow' and not a magical crow at all.

I asked the Leprechauns in Never Land what they

thought about it but they had no idea what I should do with it. I considered taking it to Ireland to see what the wizard thought but then decided that was not such a good idea. I considered Fairy Dust and the Dust of Time but I didn't know if it were dead or in suspended animation or under some kind of spell.

Finally I decided to re-animate it with a technique I learned from the Lion. It had worked before animating horses and men in the past. I tried it and the crow was immediately re-animated. The crow turned out to be a female, which I suspected because of her smaller size. She told me she was known by the name Turly, although that was not her real name. She was a sorceress and a shape shifter and she said she had brought the gift of Illusion for me. Only yesterday I had my first encounter with the concept and process of illusion. She explained that she was an illusion that is different from a dream or a vision because it was created by mind and was of mind and that my mind now had the gift of creating Illusions.

I attempted on three separate occasions to make my way to wherever and whenever Turly resided. The first two attempts were dismal failures.

The night before last my wife got up a few minutes after 4:00 o'clock in the morning. I think it was at 4:19. She turned on the light on her nightstand. I could see her out of the corner of my eye but I was completely paralyzed and unable to move even though I tried to move several times but I was unable to even make a sound.

The main field of my vision was filled with two areas of sand separated by a thin band perhaps one eighth of an inch in width which was composed of three separate layers. The central portion of this band was clear and appeared to be filled with some kind of liquid. On either side of this liquid were two separate membranes. One was almost white and the other had a bluish tint to it. The sand on the left side of the band was a light tan and composed of fine sand of uniform size, shape and color. This tan sand was fixed and immobile while the sand on the right side of the separation was multicolored, irregular grains of sand that were moving in a circulating pattern. This turned out to be extrinsic mind, the stuff that creates and comprises illusion.

On my third attempt last night, I took the Night Train at 4:00 o'clock and made it to Turly's house. It turns out that she lives in Northern France in Normandy. She was born in 1815. I met up with her in the 1850's. She lives in a three-story house made of brick with white stucco on the outside. She explained to me that she had given me the gift of illusion but that I would have to figure out how to use it. She said that the fine-grained, tan-colored sand I had encountered yesterday was actually the sands of time, while the moving particles of multicolored sand were external mind which functions outside of time and the strip that separated the two kept the two different minds apart. It would be up to me to figure out how to bridge this gap and put illusion to work. She then exposed me to separate, different illusions that were very real and lasted over two hours, from 4:00 o'clock until 6:15 a.m. What a bizarre experience that was! She explained to me that Illusion is created by extrinsic mind and affects others. When they embrace the illusion, they in turn can expand that illusion to include you. That is one way to discern that they have indeed reacted to the illusion you have created.

The difference between illusion and delusion is that illusion is created using extrinsic, or external mind. Delusion is created by one-self, using their-own internal mind. They are totally different things with completely different causes and effects.

Sleeping Buddha

Last Monday, my son called me from California and said that he thought there was something at his house. He didn't know what it was or where it was or where it had come from. He thought that they possibly picked up something while they were in Huntington Beach on Sunday. I told him that I would go over later in the evening and check it out but that I probably wouldn't get over there until after midnight.

When I went finally went over to my Son's house, I took the Facilitator, Sabatini and the Other with me. We transported over to his house a little after midnight, which would have been a little after eleven o'clock California time.

When we got there, the Other and I began

systematically going through the entire house. The Facilitator covered the back doors and Sabatini covered the front of the house. The only thing we found was located in my granddaughter's bedroom. I used the rose-colored glasses and the double-lensed pince-nez glasses as well as the reflection from the shiny surface of 'The Sword of Truth', in an attempt to visualize what we located. These all provide different perspectives to see things as they really are. All of these tools were ineffective. I knew that what I was looking for was there in that bedroom even though I couldn't see it. There was movement of air in one direction and then in the opposite direction which was billowing the curtains and clothing in a rhythmic fashion, first away from whatever was there and then towards whatever was there. There was the essence of an outline of a shape that resembled a very large meditating Buddha.

Eventually I surmised that this thing must be the mind of a Buddha and the movement of air, the breathing of a meditating Buddha. This is the first time I have encountered 'mind' as a completely separate thing. I also suspected that its nature must be super conscious. This was all novel territory for me. I had no proven strategy for dealing with the 'mind of a sleeping Buddha.' We spent almost three hours there in total before returning to my home in Arizona.

I told my son that it was probably O.K. for it to be there for the time being but that I would try to figure out a way to get rid of it. I utilized several different techniques to resolve this situation. In the end this is what I learned: This was indeed the mind of a sleeping Buddha, which existed in the early 1700's. After locating the Sleeping Buddha and visiting him several times, on one occasion his eyes were open a tiny bit. I took that to be a sign that enough of his awareness had returned that it would be safe to attempt to wake him. When I did so by touching his shoulder several times, the Buddha thanked me for waking him. He told me that he had inadvertently fallen into a deep sleep while meditating. When I asked him what he was doing in my Granddaughter's bedroom, he told me that she was in fact an old friend of his.

The next time I visited him I noticed that his long slow breathing was visible as though it were very cold inside. When I asked about his breath the Buddha told me that it was the 'Breath of Life'. I asked if I could share his 'Breath of Life, with others. He said, "Recall the memory of my breathing and you may share this 'Breath of Life' with them." When last I visited my Granddaughter's room, the mind of the Buddha had shrunk to the size of a large pear. It surrounded the small statue of the Buddha sitting on top of my granddaughter's dresser illuminated by its tiny forever-candle.

Seven Minds

I started a project approximately nine days ago, a few days before the Magical Crows came on the full moon February 22, 2016. It is said that, "Curiosity killed the cat but satisfaction brought him back." It is also said that, "Cats have nine lives." Sometimes I wonder how many lives I have left.

I saw a news clip on the TV about a young high-school girl who was an honor roll student who died after taking what she thought was LSD (lysergic acid di-ethyl amide) but was in fact a substance made in China called T-5 something. I was busy making dinner so I didn't catch her name or other details but she had such a pretty innocent face, I asked myself, "I wonder what happened to her. I wonder what kind of trouble she is in now." That is what I call curiosity.

It is always easier to find someone if you have their full name but it can still be done even without it. I found her the next morning but it did take some real effort to do so. She looked really dead. She was totally non-responsive. There was no way I was going to leave her there where I found her, in that state. Too many really bad things could happen to her. She was covered by three separate transparent layers of some kind of elastic something. I had no idea what they were so I wasn't going to take her into Never Land wrapped up like that. I ended up taking her to my house and sort of dumping her in the corner of a room. Our two corgi dogs that we have, avoided her like the plague. I assumed that sooner or later I would figure out what I needed to do to get her back on track.

A few days later, a little after midnight on the 22nd of February, I went out to the back yard to see if any Magical Crows had come yet on this, the day of the full moon. After a couple of minutes a single giant crow flew in from the north and landed on the telephone wires behind my house. It sat on the lowest wire briefly before swooping down and landing behind our Valencia orange tree. I waited a few more minutes to see if any other Magical Crows would arrive.

About five minutes later, a second crow landed briefly on the telephone wire before it too flew down and landed behind the orange tree. A few minutes later, a third Magical crow arrived staying briefly on the telephone wire before it also disappeared behind the orange tree. A fourth crow appeared, landed on the wire and then dropped down to the ground behind the orange tree. I waited patiently but no more crows arrived. After a short while all four Magical Crows hopped out from behind the orange tree in unison. Each crow had what looked like a thighbone from a chicken in its beak. They each in their turn came close to me where I sat cross-legged waiting on the brick pavers between the Jacuzzi and the swimming pool. Then, they un-ceremoniously dropped their chicken bones in a pile.

I thanked each one of the Magical Crows for their gift of what I thought were chicken bones but I had to ask them what they were for. The last of the four crows told me that they were not chicken bones but were instead petrified finger bones. The first finger bone could be used to access the past. The second finger bone was used to gain entrance into the present and the third finger bone was to be used to enter the future.

All of the four finger bones were supposed to be used as needed to rescue the dearly departed. The fourth finger bone, which was a little larger than the other three, could be used to cut a U-shaped opening into what I assumed was the enshrouding fabric of time. That would allow me to extricate the spirit of the dead person and transport it to a safe place, wherever they wanted or needed to go.

I frequently work on several different projects at the same time. Some projects are very short while others seem to overlap and be dependent on each other to finally accomplish.

Seven minds is one that is inter-related. I couldn't figure out what to do with the elastic membranes around the girl that was still in the corner of the backroom at my house. The fourth petrified finger bone would cut through the elastic membranes but then they would self heal and close up again. My assumption was that the fourth bone was used to cut a U-shaped flap in the fabric of time but this stuff didn't look like or act like, the fabric of time. I finally approached the Source and asked for information about this 'stuff'. He told me that it was not time but mind.

We had a long, drawn-out conversation about the nature of mind. This is what he told me: The Source said that there are seven (7) minds. They are:

1) The primitive mind
2) The emotional mind
3) The intellectual mind
4) The intrinsic mind
5) The extrinsic mind
6) The Spiritual mind
7) The Super conscious mind

I am familiar with the conscious mind, the subconscious mind and the super conscious mind. That adds up to only three, not seven.

I suppose I could think of the primitive mind as being the Limbic system.

I could think of the emotional mind as perhaps the pre-cortical mind.

I could think of the intellectual mind as the conscious mind.

I could think of the intrinsic mind as the subconscious mind.

I could think of the extrinsic mind as the collective consciousness of man.

I could think of the spiritual mind as that illusive thing called spirit and

I could think of the super conscious mind as the super conscious mind.

There, that's all resolved, at least to my mind.

The Source said that the three membrane-like

things that were encasing the girl, were in fact three of her fragmented minds that had been exploded by the combination of the powerful psychoactive substances that she consumed. The fourth finger bone could in fact cut through four of the seven kinds of mind. It could not cut through the primitive mind, which was totally confined to the limbic system and existed only within the confines of the physical brain itself. Also, the fourth finger bone could not cut through either the spiritual mind or the super conscious mind. The Source said that the girl died, when her primitive brain exploded from the drugs that she had taken. Those are his words, not mine, that he used to describe what happened. My task was then, to figure out how to put Humpty Dumpling back together again, when all the king's horses and all the king's men couldn't put Humpty Dumpty back together again.

I have also been working on another project for several weeks now that involved a novel approach to the healing process itself.

The first step in this process involves resetting or as it were, rebooting, the body's natural healing process.

The second step in the process involves activating or eliciting the placebo effect, which in effect is 'suspension of disbelief.'

The third step in the healing process is to identify the causative agents or events that allowed the patient to become ill in the first place and to eliminate or mitigate those factors.

The techniques that I have developed may differ

from the techniques that others might use but they are quite powerful and effective, none-the less. These techniques do not involve the use of any medications.

Once I understood the nature of this challenge and the constituents of the pliable membranes I was ready to tackle the problem. First I cut through the three layers, which must have been made up of the emotional mind, the intelligent mind and the intrinsic mind. I went through the three steps of the healing process. I rebooted the body/mind's natural healing system. Then, I energized the placebo effect and finally I regressed the young girl back in time to before she took the drugs that killed her. At that point everything began to function normally again, everything except her primitive mind. Without the primitive mind function, she could only remain dead. The membranes enveloping her vaporized and returned to their normal places and normal states. I took her to where she needed to go.

There were two doors with nothing else around. The door on the left had a sign on it that said 'Door to the Past'. The door on the right had a sign on it that said, 'Door to the Future.' She chose the door on the right because she knew the 'Door to the past' led straight to her casket. She walked through the door on the right and into another life in another time in another place. I assumed that my job was complete. But then, one never knows anything for sure.

Death's Door

I was in the third attention talking with the Source. I know that an integral step in the process of individual liberation is the establishment of an understanding or appreciation of death, not a conceptual comprehension but a personal connection with your own death. We were discussing this process. The Source suggested that I make the effort to become more familiar with this process. So, I went in search of my own death. That led me to 'Death's Door'.

The sign in large letters on the door read, Death's Door, so I entered. As I started to step through the doorway, a fly buzzed by and went ahead of me. I have never seen a fly anywhere before in non-ordinary reality. I took several steps forward, before I saw the top of a skull sticking out of the ground. The fly landed on top of the skull and the skull began to rise up out of the soil, until a full skeleton stood there in front of me. It had an ornate filigreed cross on its forehead. I sat down in front of the skeleton, with my legs crossed as if I were going to meditate. The skeleton copied my movements and sat down on the ground in front of me. I reached out and removed the cross on its forehead and put it on my own forehead. This left a hole in the shape of a cross in the forehead of the skeleton.

I told the skeleton that I wasn't afraid of death. It just stared straight out at me from those empty eye sockets. I told him that I had unfinished business that I needed to attend to. He remained motionless and continued to stare. I told him that I needed some cash, a lot of cash to settle my debts. He moved his head slowly up and down, in acknowledgement. I continued with my list of unfinished goals. He listened intently.

I said I would like to become a proficient healer. He reached out and touched my forehead where the cross that was taken from his forehead now rested. Then I said I would like to become a great seer. He reached out with both hands and touched both of my eyes. I said I would like to fulfill the responsibilities of the Oracle and he reached out and touched my lips. I said that I didn't want to become deaf like my grandfather had been and he reached out and put his hands on my ears. I said that I didn't want to have heart problems and he reached out and put his right hand on my chest. I said that I didn't want to be unable to get around on my own two feet and he reached out and touched my legs.

Then he reached out with both of his hands and held my hands and stared intently into my face for an extended period of time. He stood up. Then sank slowly back into the ground. The fly flew off of the top of his head and landed on my right shoulder, as the last remnants of the skeleton's skull sank beneath the sand.

The fly remained on my right shoulder as I returned to the third attention where I shared my experiences with the Source. The Source thought for a moment then said, "Few have managed to make such a deal with their death."

I asked the Source for its blessing for this journey that I was just beginning.

He said, "You have always had my blessing." Then, he vanished completely, leaving the fly and I alone, there in the third attention.

This is an appropriate time to clarify my use of the term 'Attention'. Everyone has heard the words, "Pay Attention!" That is an act of volition, a request to notice or to be aware or to be actively engaged in and with whatever is transpiring in that place and in that time. The 'first attention' is our awareness of the physical world in which we live and function.

The 'second attention' is the realm of the sorcerer, which includes the dreamscape. The 'Attention' is not the place but your awareness of and your functionality within that arena of reality. Sorcerers believe that the 'second attention' serves as a bridge to the 'third attention'.

The 'third attention' is your awareness and your functionality within that arena where the spirits and Gods reside.

There are other 'attentions' that correlate with other things like, Insanity, health and healing as well as many others. These other 'attentions' exist. Access to them is possible but the eye cannot see what the mind does not know and does not understand.

Tytus

In the pursuit of more specific information from my death, I embarked on five or six excursions through 'Death's Door' last night. Each time I would make my way to the place where the skeleton was buried in sand with only the very top of its skull sticking out above the surface. Each time, I would sit down in front of the skull with my legs crossed as though I were going to meditate. Each time, the golden fly, which is the symbol or representation of my personal death, would leave my right shoulder and land on top of the skull, the skeleton would slowly rise up out of the sand until it was standing erect on its two feet, then it would sit down facing me with its legs crossed, as we sat almost nose to nose. Each time, I would ask as many questions as I could, before I fell off the wagon, meaning before I went to sleep at the switch.

The skeleton has never spoken to me. We communicate with yes or no questions, signs or gestures and head shakes. When I got around to asking that specific question regarding his ability to speak, he shook his head sideways, pointed at where his voice box should have been with the index finger of his left hand, then shook his hand sideways back and forth with his index finger pointed straight upward.

What I learned during these five or six exchanges was the following: He confirmed that he was my death. The sand he was buried in is the 'Sands of Time' and that is what allows my awareness its ability to travel through time and space and for me to do all of the other strange things which I do, like communicate with the dead, travel to the dead zone, see the future and the past and understand and function within the event horizon. He confirmed that his name was Tytus. That was the first name I presented to him as a possibility but I have no Idea how I came up with that name or where that name came from. I have never even heard of that name. He also said that his being my death has allowed me to do what very few can ever do and that is, to see and to communicate with other people's deaths.

After our last discussion ended, he leaned forward, gave me a hug from our sitting positions, stood up slowly before sinking slowly back beneath the Sands of Time, until only the very top of his head still appeared. The fly left the top of Tytus' skull, landed on my shoulder and then we departed.

The next night I went through Death's Door two more times. The first time, after Tytus had come out of the sand and was sitting directly in front of me, he reached out with two fingers on his right hand and placed them on my forehead. He left them there for a short while and then we were able to communicate telepathically.

He told me that the freedom I had to do all of these strange things came with the price of having to be personally responsible for not getting myself terminated. He was indisposed and would not be with me constantly protecting me from dying before it was my time. All of the decisions that I made would be mine and mine alone, for better or for worse. The fly would offer no protection at all. It would only be there as the constant reminder that I flew alone in darkness or in light.

The Golden Fly

A couple of nights ago I was awake staring at the ceiling, so I decided to revisit my own personal death. To get there I went to the door marked "Death's Door." As I opened the door, the golden fly on my left shoulder flew in ahead of me and landed on top of the exposed bony cranium sticking out of the sand. When the fly landed on the skull, it began to raise up out of the sand, first the head, then the torso and finally the legs, as the sand drained out of the eye sockets and out from in between the vertebra. The upright skeleton, which is my own personal death, is several inches taller than I. It stared down at me in total silence. The golden fly is actually an icon, a surrogate for my death. My death stays buried beneath the sands of time, instead of doing his job of watching after my personal safety and well being, until the actual moment of my death, when it is supposed to escort me to whatever fate awaits me.

My death has never spoken a single word to me before. Tonight I came in search of information about my own death. A prime objective for every sorcerer is to establish a personal relationship with death. I asked my death if it would answer a question, should I propose one? Death shook its head slowly from side to side. I asked if it would answer yes or no, if I guessed something correctly. Again Death shook its head slowly from side to side. I tried another approach. If I guessed something correctly, would it shake its head up and down for a yes or from side to side for a no? Finally my death relented and agreed to this arrangement, feeling confident that I couldn't possibly guess anything correctly. Great, but I had no idea what to ask. There is a state of mind where purposeful information can flow from one person's mind, into another person's mind. It isn't always easy to get into that state of mind but I have done it before. So, I gave it a go, and this is what transpired.

    The first word that came to mind was the name Robert, so I asked my death if his name were Robert. Death moved his bony skull slowly up and down. The next word that popped into my mind was the name Kleiner, or Kleinin. So I posed that question. Was his name Kleiner, or Kleinin? Again death moved his head up and down but even more slowly than before. Next, I clearly saw a young girl whose facial features resembled those of my death. I asked my death if he had a daughter. He hesitated before affirming with a nod of his head. The name Cherylin came to me. A name I have never even heard of before. I asked if that were his daughter's name. He stared at me intently from those empty eye sockets before giving me a single nod. "Your daughter's name was Cherylin Kleinin." I said. Next, I saw water flowing in onto the floor, coming from every direction. This was obviously a flood of some kind. I blurted out, "Your daughter drowned in a flood. Your only daughter drowned in a flood. Your wife drowned in that flood. Your only wife drowned in that flood." His stare was long and painful. There was no answer needed. I knew that was what happened. He knew that I knew what he was thinking. After all, he was my death. We were connected until death do us part.

My last comments remained unanswered. "You lived to be very old. You lived to be ninety-seven. You never married again. You grew bitter and very angry. That is why you now spend all of your time buried beneath the sands of time, living there in your memories. That is why I have such a propensity for the dreamscape and for time travel.

The Ram's Horn

After the progress I made with Death the night before last, I returned to see what, if any, additional progress might be possible. Death was not buried in the sand for the first time. I asked if he were Jewish because Kleiner seems to frequently be a Jewish family name but I had never encountered the name Kleinin before? To my surprise, my Death spoke to me for the first time.

He said that his family name was Kleiner but it was changed at Ellis Island when his family emigrated to Kleinin and so it remained. He told me that his wife's name was Rachel. After she and their daughter tragically perished in the great flood, he became very bitter. He stopped going to Temple and he cursed God for his terrible loss. He lived a very long life, acquired great wealth but he never found happiness and never had a single friend. His punishment for his blasphemy was a long life in misery and to become my personal death and made to be responsible for an idiot like me. Those are his words, not mine. I told him that there was a place I knew of that he should visit and I could take him there. Death left the Golden Fly in charge there behind Death's Door, then Death extended his bony hand and I escorted him to meet Abraham.

There were thirteen three-legged stools arranged in a circle around a fourteenth stool in its center. I introduced Robert to Abraham. He invited Robert to sit down on the fourteenth stool in the middle of the circle. He picked up the ram's horn and blew a long wailing note. Out of nowhere appeared a bearded shepherd with a curved knife in the sash around his waist. Abraham said to the shepherd, "Levi, this is Robert. He is from the lost tribe of Israel." Levi embraced Robert. He hugged him first on the right cheek then he hugged him on the left cheek and said, "Welcome, brother."

Abraham continued blowing the ram's horn again and again and again. Each time another shepherd appeared, one for each of the twelve tribes of Israel. Each welcomed Robert with a hug on the right cheek and then a hug on the left cheek and then a 'Welcome, brother.' After twelve of the stools were filled and the circle nearly complete, Abraham again blew the ram's horn a long and sorrowful note. And Rachel appeared. She embraced the bones of Robert and he became whole. No longer was he a skeleton but a handsome young man dressed in shepherd's clothing, absent the knife. Rachel took her place on the fourteenth stool in the center of the circle where Robert had sat, as Robert took his rightful place on the thirteenth stool, the missing thirteenth tribe of Israel.

Abraham blew the ram's horn one last time and Robert's daughter Cherylin emerged from the ether and embraced her parents. They remained together in the center of the circle as one by one, each of the heads of the twelve tribes of Israel disappeared into their past. The last things to disappear were the fourteen stools, the ram's horn and Abraham, the father of the Jewish people.

We were left there alone, Robert, Rachel, Cherylin and I. When Robert and I finally returned, after they said their farewells, Robert remained that robust young man in his prime, still wearing his shepherd's clothing. He was no longer a skeleton buried in the sands of time but Death, my personal Death. His job is to keep me safe and sound until it is my time to die, my time to depart.

Car Seventeen

This morning I was working on another project when I checked the clock. It was 4:01 a.m. I ran outside in hopes that the Night Train had not yet departed. The engineer waved to me as I ran towards the train. The conductor yelled, "Where you headed?" I shouted back that I had no idea. He said, "car seventeen" then yelled, "All aboard" at the top of his lungs.

I ran up the three steps into the first car right behind the coal car. No one was in there. The first car is always full of something but my eyes usually need some help to be able to see what is there when it actually appears to be empty. The first thing I tried was the rose-colored glasses. They provided no help. Then, I put on the double-lensed pince-nez spectacles. There was still nothing to be seen. When I looked into the reflection from the Sword of Truth my eye caught a tiny glint from the far end of the passenger car. It turned out to be the Golden Fly.

With the aid of those rose-colored glasses and double-lensed pince-nez spectacles and the reflection from the Sword of Truth all combined I could clearly see Robert, my own Personal Death, sitting in the last seat on the left hand side at the far end of the passenger car. As I walked down the isle towards my death he asked where I was going. I told Robert that the conductor told me to go to car seventeen. Robert asked me if I always do what someone tells me to do. I thought about that before responding, "Not too often but the conductor has never given me bad advice before"

Robert suggested that I check on the next car before jumping the gun in my haste to get to car seventeen. I opened the door slowly just to be safe. There were no other cars. The wind whipped me around, as the steel tracks receded rapidly into the distance at an ever-increasing rate of speed. I closed the door quickly with a look of real surprise on my face. Robert then suggested that I check for the coal car. When I opened the front door of our car I was in for an even bigger surprise because the coal car and the engine were both missing. Yet the car we were riding in continued gaining speed. Robert smiled at me and said, "You are on a run-away train riding with your own personal death and you have no idea where you are going. That sounds just great."

A small gambling table materialized out of thin air in the middle of the isle between us as the rocketing train hurtled onward towards nowhere. A single deck of playing cards adorned the tabletop. Robert said, "Black Jack!" I wasn't sure what he meant exactly but he took a single card from the top of the deck and placed it face down on the table in front of him. I did the same.

The next card he took he placed face up. It was the queen of diamonds. I followed his lead and took my second card, turned it over and placed it onto the table face up. It was the queen of hearts. He took his third card. It was the king of diamonds. I took my third card. It was the king of hearts. And so it continued. Robert took his fourth card. It was the ace of Diamonds. My fourth card was the ace of hearts. Robert took his fifth and final card. It was the jack of diamonds. My fifth card was the Jack of hearts.

Robert gave me a sly grin as he turned over his first card, which had been face down. It was the Ace of spades. He smiled with his big toothy smile.

I turned over my first card that had been face down and placed it in order next to my queen, my king, my ace and my jack. It was the ten of hearts.

Everything disappeared in a flash. I was back in my bed. The numerals on the face of the clock glowed red, 4:13 a.m.

I had just survived a gamble with my death on a runaway train bound for nowhere and lived to tell the tale. My death had come up short with his pair of aces against my straight, royal flush of hearts.

Stacking the deck can be a tricky affair, especially when playing five-card stud with your own personal death.

Talkin'... Robin...

On the 11th of September America experienced a great tragedy.

On the 11th of August we Americans experienced a great loss.

We lost our "Talkin'... Robin...Williams"

He meant so much to so many. He was my wife's favorite actor. He was my favorite comedian. He was America's gift to the world of joy and laughter. His legacy will live forever in our hearts. America's strength lies not in gospel or decree but in our mirth and laughter. He embodied the heart and soul of the American spirit.

Monday night, on the 11th of August, I summoned Robin's spirit but to no avail. So, I went looking for him. It took a great deal of time and a great deal of effort but I finally found him on the sidewalk near a busy street, totally out of it. He was sitting on the sidewalk with his legs stretched out in front of him, leaning against a light pole. His head was slumped down onto his chest. He was wearing what looked like an old engineer's cap, limp and badly faded, from some far off time and far away places. Nothing I did seemed to have any effect on him. He was out, O-U-T...OUT.

It took me three separate trips over just to get him on his feet. Once he was upright and semi standing, I opened a portal and we transported into my back yard. I put him down on one of the two lounges we have near the swimming pool. I checked on him periodically. Tuesday night I checked on him several more times but he was still totally out of it.

Early Wednesday morning, around 4:30 a.m., I checked on him again. He started to revive enough that with help, he could actually sit upright in the lounge chair.

After several efforts, I managed to get him to actually stand upright on his own, without my assistance. I helped him to walk around a little bit to clear his head of the cobwebs. He noticed the tall man who was still sleeping in the other lounge chair next to him.

Robin stopped and stared at the sleeping man in the

lounge chair and asked, "Who is that? He is really tired!"

I told Robin that the sleeping man in the other lounge chair was my own personal death.

Without a moment's hesitation, Robin retorted, "He is dead tired… and tired of being dead!"

I knew then that our Robin Williams would be O.K. Rockin'… Talkin'…Robin perchance shall see "What Dreams May Come!"

Night Train to Heaven

Thursday morning early, I went out to the back yard to check on Robin. He was sitting with his legs crossed on the cool deck near the swimming pool picking at a guitar. He seemed safe enough for the time being. Later in the morning at 3:57 a.m., I went back outside to check on his status once again. He was strumming his guitar and quietly singing a tune. I asked Robin if he was up to going on an adventure? He said that he was. The Night Train would be coming by in three minutes. I asked Robin to bring his guitar. We still had time to catch the Night Train. I also told him that he had to have a destination in mind because the conductor would ask him where he wanted to go.

The Night Train chugged to a stop directly in front of us. It was this huge black steam engine with all the noises, smoke & steam that accompany one. The massive coal car behind the engine connected directly to the first passenger car. The conductor stood on the ground at its entrance and called loudly over the hissing steam and grumbling boiler, as smoke continued to boil up into the night air from its smoke stack. "Aboard... All aboard...Tickets... Tickets please." Robin shrugged his shoulders and looked shocked as he turned his empty palms skyward. We had no tickets. I said, "Tell him where you want to go." To my surprise, Robin yelled over the whistle from the train, "Heaven. Take me to Heaven. I always wanted to go to Heaven."

As we clambered up the four steps into the first passenger car next to the coal car, the conductor yelled, "Car 21." Robin asked the conductor if we could just wait for car 21 to come by? The conductor told us, "No. Everyone has to come on board through this entrance, no exceptions." Robin looked resolutely at the coal car and retorted, "I sure wouldn't want to ride in that car. It's going to hell for sure."

The first passenger car with row after row of parallel wooden seats reminiscent of church pews was totally empty. Robin looked around at all the empty seats and blurted out, "No one's here, we must be headed for Heaven."

As we made our way back through several sleeper cars, he said, "Everyone must be dead or sleeping."

When we passed through the lounge car, with its empty tables and long wooden bar, stocked with all the booze you could imagine, he mumbled, "I could easily fall off of the wagon in here."

The dining car was spectacular, but it too was devoid

of patrons. Robin fingered the tablecloths and napkins, and commented, "Nice linen. I probably shouldn't cop any silverware since I'm trying to get in to Heaven."

Car 21 was the last car in the train. It wasn't a double decker but it was elevated a few feet, with lots of glass for observation. As soon as we got through car 21, the train stopped and we got off. There was nothing but white sand as far as you could see in every direction. The train and its tracks disappeared. We were left alone and deserted. Robin looked around and said, "This is the biggest beach I have ever seen. Too bad there is no water and where are all the people?"

I left him there, in heaven, sitting in the sand, playing his guitar.

Robin's Return

I checked the back yard later in the morning. Robin was sitting next to the Jacuzzi playing his acoustic guitar and singing softly to himself. I asked him how things had gone in heaven. He told me that there was too much beach, no water and no people. His heaven had not turned out so well. He said it was like being in the middle of the Sahara desert in the middle of summer. I told him that it wasn't safe for him to remain in my back yard. So, I took him to Never Land and introduced him to all of the people who reside there including Vanessa, the girl who recently arrived after being killed and then pursued by her ex-husband.

When we crossed over the bridge into Never Land Robin said, "Now this is more like it. This is real heaven." It is very beautiful there and it is also filled with many wonderful, magical creatures.

The next evening I returned to Never Land to check on Robin and Vanessa. I was told that it was 'Love at first sight' for Robin and for Vanessa. They were inseparable and talked incessantly. I have to admit that Vanessa was very attractive with her red, red, hair and her white, white, skin. They disappeared into the forest and would return during the daytime to play with the children, the bears and the talking lions.

They had a tiny tent in the forest where they spent nights together. In front of the tent they had an everlasting fire pit that never needed tending and never needed more wood and never produced any smoke, only warmth and a constantly flickering campfire. Vanessa told me that her husband's wrath was so powerful that it followed her even in death and kept her bound with ropes and clothed in shame. She had sought help from all of her friends and family. Only the anger of Vanessa's cousin, when she was murdered, was powerful enough and focused enough to free her for brief periods of time by burning through the ropes that imprisoned her, thus the origin of 'the smell of smoke' her cousin occasionally experienced.

Robin told me that after he had heart surgery he was never the same. During the surgery they saved his life but he lost his edge. His brain would no longer function at lightning speed. He had lost his timing and he knew that his comedic life had suffered irreparable damage. The issue of the Parkinson's diagnosis was the final nail in his comedic coffin. He was honest with himself and he knew the time had come to take that 'final bow'.

They both told me they wanted to return to another earthly life together. I told them that they were welcome to stay in Never Land together as long as they chose to do so. I told them I could take them anywhere they chose to go. But I didn't know how to re-incarnate them back into the world of the living. That was something they would have to talk to God about.

Cousins

I was finally able to talk with Vanessa for the first time early this morning at 5:30 a.m. Robin was still sleeping. We sat down by the smokeless fire in the everlasting fire pit in front of their tiny tent. There were so many unanswered questions that I had about this whole scenario. I always try to keep an open mind but I know that my own personal perspectives often intrude into this process.

I became involved personally with Vanessa's story when her cousin, who has worked with me for twenty years, complained incessantly about smelling smoke in all kinds of places and at all different times when no one else smelled smoke and there was no identifiable source for the smoke she was smelling. When she began bringing jars of Vicks Vapor Rub to the office and stuffing it up her nose, my curiosity was aroused.

I summoned the 'Gift of the Oracle' in an effort to dispel the problem of Vanessa's cousin smelling smoke. Thus was created: 'October Sky', 'A Curse Is Just A Curse' and 'The Fourth Vision'. The problem with her Smelling Smoke dissipated but I knew there had to be more to this story.

The string of clues:

Her cousin, Vanessa, was murdered. Vanessa's estranged husband stabbed her several times and slit her throat with a knife.

Vanessa's cousin was subsequently stopped by a highway patrol. He thought he saw Vanessa riding as the passenger sitting next to her in the passenger's seat of her car.

The smell from the smoke grew stronger over time for Vanessa's cousin. To her cousin, the smell was reminiscent of cigar smoke but she didn't know any of relatives who smoked cigars.

I obtained permission to intrude into this story from Vanessa's cousin. I summoned Vanessa. She arrived next to my bed in very bad condition. Her hands were bound with several wrappings of rope, knotted several times very tightly, with a long piece trailing back dragging on the ground behind her. This made a loud scuffing noise as she approached. She was wearing a pair of men's jeans that were way too large for her. The legs were too long and this added to the shuffling sounds because they completely covered her feet. Her hair was totally messed up and covered with dried blood. Her face and arms were also splattered all over with clotted blood and there was a gapping wound across her entire throat. She had been wandering aimlessly for many months in this terrible condition. She was still wearing the top part of a baby doll pajamas.

I took Vanessa into Never Land and asked some of the people there to take care of her while I went to get a surgeon to care for her. I introduced Vanessa to her caregivers and to her surgeon. I left them to care for her needs while she recovered. It had been about ten days since she first arrived in Never Land. I would check on her progress daily. This was the first opportunity that I have had to talk with her, since she arrived. I had many questions for her. I knew that she was the missing component of this entangled story.

Rescue Mission

On Tuesday Flight 4U9525 with 150 persons on board crashed into the side of a mountain in France. On Friday night, I went over there to rescue as many of the deceased as I could. At that time it was thought that the co-pilot might have deliberately crashed the aircraft into the mountainside. I escorted the dearly departed in groups of twos and threes to the closest church. It took awhile but I kept a close count of the numbers of passengers that I escorted away from the crash site. I eventually took one hundred and forty nine souls to the church where I told them to stay put. I would return for them later. The co-pilot, I left him sitting on a rock on the hillside.

On Saturday night I went out to wait for the 'Night Plane' to arrive at 1:00 a.m. in the morning. The engine sounds coming from the approaching airplane weren't familiar to me. They were definitely coming from an internal combustion aircraft engine but they sounded a little different. When the plane landed and taxied up to my driveway, it was definitely not an airplane that I was familiar with. It had a single high-wing, with one engine on its nose and a tail wheel. It was a small passenger plane of some kind. I went around to the far side of the aircraft to where the entrance door was located and climbed on board. This was definitely a passenger plane. It had two rows of five seats down each side of the fuselage. There was a narrow pathway between the two rows of seats. Up in the cabin, there were two seats for pilots. The only person in the aircraft was the captain seated in the left front seat. I made my way up to the front and sat down in the co-pilot's seat on the right side of the cabin. The captain looked familiar. When I mentioned that to him, he informed me that he was the captain of the Airbus A 320 that had recently crashed into the mountainside in France. He said he was going to rescue the others from the plane crash, so I accompanied him. It took us fifteen separate trips but we were able to transport all of the passengers from the church in France to a location in Dusseldorf, Germany. The captain was very polite and repeatedly apologized to his passengers for the inconvenience of them all having been killed. The last thing we did was go back to the crash site. The captain was looking for something but he didn't say what it was. The copilot was still there. He was complaining loudly that he was freezing and starving to death and no one was helping him. We both ignored his pleas for assistance. He was whining about having a broken leg and being unable to walk.

On Sunday night, when I went out to await the arrival of the 'Night Plane' I heard the distinct sound of a V-1 buzz-bomb coming, then passing over head and then trailing off into the distance. It approached from the west and departed to the east. No plane landed that night. That was the first time that has ever occurred. I was curious about the source of the sound of the V-1 buzz bomb. The solution that I dreamed up was to travel back in time and then to transport to the source of the pulse jet noise. I had never transported backwards in time, then transported into or onto a fast moving object like that before but I thought that it could be done.

The object turned out to be a small single-seat fighter plane powered by a pulse jet engine. Later, I did a search on Google and discovered that the Germans had made two such experimental aircraft. The first was powered by a V-1 pulse jet engine, the second powered by a larger pulse jet engine that produced eleven hundred pounds of thrust. The cockpit was very small and cramped. It contained only a basic instrument panel. The larger model had two machine guns in its nose. The one that I was in had only one.

The next night, (Monday night) when I went outside to wait for the night plane, I heard this really, really loud airplane fly over, turn into cross wind, then onto the down wind leg. I knew that it must be really big and have multiple engines propelling it to be making that much noise. It turned out to be a German Arado 232 transport plane, with four large radial engines that had made all of that noise. When I got inside of the transport plane, the only person there was the same captain from the A 320 Airbus. He told me he was going to pick up the passengers and crew in Dusseldorf and transport them to their final destination. We picked up every one where we had left them in a hanger at the airport in Dusseldorf and transported them to a place I have never been before.

The Arado 232, with all of the passengers and crew from the ill-fated Airbus A 320 with the exception of the copilot Arrianis Lubix, landed in an endless, open space that was light tan, slightly darker than the color of sand. The cloudless sky was an even lighter tan. There was absolutely nothing anywhere. After everyone deplaned, this very tall, female figure appeared. She was nine or ten feet tall and was dressed in a short sleeve, gold-colored, silk blouse and a long, floor-length tapered skirt with a gold decoupage-covered surface. The skirt never seemed to move and so it appeared to be made of something solid, like metal. She held a large stack of papers cradled in her left arm and was systematically distributing them. Each distribution was about a quarter of an inch thick. The recipients would open them and shortly thereafter, would vanish into thin air, without a trace. When the captain received his, it looked like the script for a movie or a play. On its cover page was the date 1308 AD in large print. There was also a person's name along with other information. He vanished before I could get a clear view of his script. After everyone else had vanished, the plane also disappeared. That left only this tall female, who subsequently was identified as the 'Assignment Angel', and myself standing alone facing each other. She had one remaining script in her hand. She stretched her long thin arm out to me to deliver the 'assignment'. I graciously took it from her. On its cover page was:

Name:JEROME BROWN
Date:AD 1107
Title: Cobbler
Location: Town of Londonderry
One wife:Margaritte
Children:Three

I lifted that thick first page exposing an ancient brass key, the key to a new life's experience, in another time and in another place. This must have been intended for the co-pilot, Andreas Gunter Lubitz. I blurted out, "But I'm not dead!" The angel instantly disintegrated into a thousand pieces that fell to the floor in a pile. I dropped the script I was holding and transported back to my own life, to my own house, to my own time.

The next night I went out again to wait for the night plane to come at 1:00 o'clock in the morning. Out of the night sky fell this object, 'Thwack' right onto the asphalt street in front of my foot, so I stooped down and picked it up. It was that same script from the night before but it was wrapped up in a protective plastic covering. A few moments later a two-place glider silently touched down at the end of my street and rolled to a dead stop in front of my driveway. I jumped into the back seat of what looked, in the dim light, like a two place Switzer glider. The thing began moving forward immediately, accelerating swiftly as though being towed by an invisible tow plane. In no time we were circling above the crash site. I assumed that the Assignment Angel intended for me to drop the plastic wrapped script of a new life down to the co-pilot. But there was no way that I was going to get involved by doing that. It wasn't my place to judge his actions and it wasn't my place to provide him with another life. The glider circled around several times before it returned me to my home. The whole process took less than half an hour.

I wasn't sure exactly what I should do with the life experience that I carried under my arm. I certainly was not going to give it to Lubitz. I got the bright idea of offering the new life to Robin Williams who had been hiding from his many demons at my house since shortly after his death. He and his girl friend, Vanessa Ortega, wanted to share a new life together in a place where their tormentors couldn't find them. Until now

I had no idea how to accomplish that task. I offered Robin that new life as a cobbler in the 12th century but he would not accept a new life without Vanessa. I told them I was going to take the 'Night Bus' back to where the Assignment Angel was, to return this cobbler's life to her, and that they were welcome to come along for the ride with me. Perhaps they could talk her into giving them a new life together, somewhere in time. They both knew that once they left the protection of the place that I had created for them, their Demons would soon overtake them. They waited until the last possible moment to decide. We barely made it to the street in time as the 'Night Bus' came rolling down the road.

    I introduced Robin and Vanessa to Brad raccoon the bus driver and asked if he could take us to where the Assignment Angel was located. I showed Brad the rope I had used to secure both of them to me, so they wouldn't get lost somewhere in time. He chuckled to himself under his breath and mumbled, "Good Luck with those two." through his pointy little raccoon teeth. In a flash we burst out onto the desolate tan earth and sky scape where only the Appointment Angel remained. I told her their story. She gave them each a new script and they disappeared into thin air, holding hands and laughing like a couple of young kids with their first love.

    That giant Assignment Angel turned to me with a frown on her face. She obviously wasn't accustomed to not having her way. I returned the cobbler's life script to her, still bound up in heavy plastic and said with a sly grin on my face, "Perhaps you have just witnessed the creation of 'The Ghost of Gunter Mountain'."

Everything vanished in an instant and I once again found myself standing alone under the street lamp in front of my house. It was 2:17 a.m. in the morning.

Abu Dhabi

This morning I had a normal dream, a dream like you or anyone else might have. I only remember a normal dream if I am in the process of waking up, which I was. I was waking up because I needed to go to the bathroom. That is something I need to do every night.

In that dream my wife and I were in a hotel room somewhere but I don't know where. I had just hung up the phone after arranging for our airline tickets for us to return back home after vacationing. I told my wife that we had our seats for the flight back home tomorrow. I got up out of bed and went to the bathroom. When I returned I checked the time on the clock on the nightstand next to the bed. It was 3:58 in the morning. I was really tired but I thought I should at least check on the Night Train that comes by at 4:00 o'clock every morning.

I went out to the street in front of our house. The Night Train was just pulling up when I got there. I had no idea where I should be going and I had no ticket anyway. The conductor yelled, "All aboard." I was the only person there. When I told the conductor that I had no ticket, I turned my empty hand over palm up to show him and written in dark purple ink, in what was this beautiful cursive writing were the words, Abu Dhabi. He said, "First car."

I climbed the three steps up and got on board the Night Train. The car appeared to be completely empty. I put on the magic double lensed pince-nez spectacles and I could see that the car was full of recently dead persons headed somewhere. The only empty seat that I saw was at the far end of the train car in the very last row. I made my way back past all the sad faces and sat down in the only vacant seat. But, before I could engage the passenger next to me in conversation, the train jerked to a stop and the conductor yelled, "Abu Dhabi" and everyone started leaving the train. I fell in line and followed the other sojourners out of the train. As they walked past a pile of luggage, each retrieved their own belongings. I asked the uniformed monitor supervising luggage retrieval what was going on, he said that each of the travelers was retrieving their personal memories. I was last in line and by the time I reached the place where the luggage had been piled, nothing was left for me.

The line snaked its way towards another uniformed person at the other end of the line. He was handing out scrolls tied with a yellow ribbon to each and every one of the people who had been on the train. As each person accepted their own scroll, they were whisked away by some invisible force and disappeared without a trace. When I got to the end of the line, the man had already handed out his last scroll. He looked up at me with a startled face and then, everything there disintegrated leaving me alone back in my bed looking up at the blank ceiling. I looked at the clock. It was 4:05 a.m.

Yesterday a 'Dubai Air' airliner had crashed with sixty-two Russian vacationers on board, killing all passengers instantly before they had time to retrieve any of their memories. I had just witnessed each of those passengers gather their personal memories and begin their new lives in another place, somewhere in time.

Ashes...Ashes...We All Fall down!

I just returned from California. I was walking the four blocks to my home from where the shuttle left me there at the shuttle station. On the curb, by the side of the house directly across the street from my house, I noticed a small wooden box with a domed lid. It looked like a tiny sea trunk about four inches long and two and one half inches wide and maybe three inches high. The outside was covered in decoupage with colorful religious symbols. I was pulling my suitcase and I had a black leather backpack on my shoulders but that didn't keep me from bending down as I walked by scooping up the small chest and opening it. Someone's crumbly ashes spilled out onto my hand. The chest was filled to overflowing with someone. I immediately closed the lid on the chest and put it back on the curb where I found it. I hoped no one would follow me home and

I hoped no one would take a few of their lost crumbs, personally. It did seem to me to be an odd place to put someone's final remains...there on the curb like that. It's almost like being dumped on the curb by someone who had had it with this whole storage thing.

Curiosity got the better of me. I summoned the deceased owner of these ashes. Her name was Rachel, Rachel Contreras. She told me that she was ninety-seven when she died and that she was born in 1906 in Mexico. That would indicate that she probably passed away in 2003. I asked Rachel how old she was now. She said that she was forty-seven. Rachel appeared to me to be a very old and weathered forty-seven year-old female. Her complexion was very dark and sunburned. She told me her mother was a native Indian and her father was a Spaniard. That explained her sharp facial features, with high cheekbones and sharp pointed nose. Rachel was busy working quickly with her long deft fingers on a small earthen pot. She told me that her mother had made pottery but she herself never had time to do that when she was living because of the nine children she bore. She showed me where she gathered clay from the streambeds and where she gathered wood to fire her kiln. Rachel showed me rows of small finished clay pots with their matching lids, all filled with ashes from her deceased relatives.

Rachel seemed not to be bothered by someone leaving her ashes on a curb or by me spilling some of them on my hand. Incidentally, I did wash my hands very well with soap and water as soon as I got inside of my house. It seems that I was the only one having a problem with this ashes thing. Obviously it didn't bother Rachel and may well have not bothered the person who left the ashes on the curb. At least it was better than being tossed into the trashcan somewhere for a one-way ride to the city dump.

These ashes gave me pause, to question not only my own personal perspective with respect to death and dying and being dead but also those of society at large. Since I communicate with the deceased on a regular basis, my personal reactions to this event could have been very jaded but it wasn't. When one is unexpectedly confronted by 'Death' in any form, we tend to react with a preprogrammed, hard-wired response.

That response should be one of respect. It should be one with dignity for the departed, no matter what the circumstance, no matter what the cause. By the same token, we should extend to all living things the same respect and dignity that every living thing deserves whether they are alive or deceased. We should extend to every other living thing the respect we would expect from them at the time of our own death.

Dust to dust…Ashes to ashes… We will all fall down!

Battleship Blue

I woke up a little before 2:00 o'clock in the morning and went outside in front of the house to see what was happening. Instead of seeing our deserted street lit up by a street lamp I found myself looking down through the fog at a battleship far below from several thousand feet in the air above. It was much smaller than the Battleship Missouri but I still think it was a battleship. The forward turret had three large gun barrels protruding out from it. The turret was turned at ninety degrees to the long axis of the ship and all three guns were fired simultaneously at some distant target.

The next instant I was standing on the deck of the ship next to the forward turret. The deck was deserted. The battleship was not painted Battleship Gray, like an American ship, but a much bluer gray. I assumed that this must be a ship from another navy.

The next instant I was standing on a dirt pathway looking at a young boy pulling a wagon with several bottles of milk in it. He was about nine years old and was dressed in shorts with straps running over his shoulders. He had on short white socks and low-cut, brown leather shoes. The grass was green and the deciduous trees all had plenty of green foliage, so it must have been summer.

Then, I was in a cottage. In front of me there stood a young woman of about thirty years. She was standing at the sink holding up a large piece of cheesecloth examining it in front of the light coming in from the window. She was wearing a long gray homespun wool dress. I heard the whistling sound of the supersonic incoming shells from the battleship hidden far away, cloaked in the misty fog. War had descended upon France shattering the peaceful countryside.

As I walked down the rutted muddy road passing burned out shells of barns and dilapidated houses, leafless trees and barren fields, limping and dragging an injured foot, I turned down a familiar path from my past, a past barely remembered. The picket fence no longer white, barely there, with wide sections long since burned for warmth from harsh lonely winters. I tried to remember. I tried to remember the songs of summer, the smell of warm milk, the taste of fresh cheese but I still smelled of diesel fuel and burnt cordite, cigarettes and rotting flesh.

"How old am I? How old was I then? Was there ever a then? Is there even a now? Who am I? What have I done, in the name of country, in the name of family, in the name of God? Is there a God? How could God let this happen? What have they done? What have we done? What have I done...what have I done?"

The old cow, black and white, stares at me from in between the rails in the split rail fence, slowly chewing her cud. She just stares at me, as if she knows.

I rock slowly back and forth in the old rocking chair I made from that broken down picket fence long ago, or was it long ago? I look down at my frail thin hands, with their splintered nails and missing finger. "Did I do those things, long ago... long ago?

I wonder if God will remember? I wonder if God will forgive me? I wonder if I can forgive myself? Perhaps I deserve a medal? Perhaps!

I remember...I remember now...I remember you... But do you remember me?

The old cow knows. She knows. The old cow knows. She just doesn't say."

The Hitch Hiker

This morning after I made a bathroom run, I checked the clock on my nightstand. It was 3:45 a.m. I grabbed the old leather suitcase and ran out to the street in front of our house. There was nothing happening there. The streetlight punctuated the night's silence. Even the bugs were sound asleep. I stood in the street facing non-existent oncoming traffic and instinctively stuck out my right arm and waved my thumb back and forth, heading east. A 1949 Dodge Desoto materialized out of nowhere and stopped to offer me a ride.

The driver asked where I was headed. I responded, "East" and hopped in. I tossed my empty old suitcase onto the back seat and we headed east. The driver looked familiar but I couldn't place him right off. The Desoto wasn't new. The paint was a faded maroon. The headliner was intact. That's always a good sign that the car had not been abused. The muffler sounded O.K. The brakes didn't squeak and the gears all seemed to mesh. We made small talk for a while but I still wasn't able to put a name to his face.

The triangular wing windows were open and slanted forward scooping fresh air from outside into the car. The back window on the passenger side was cracked open for ventilation. These old cars didn't come with seat belts or air conditioning. You had to just make do. I could still smell the rubber from the old floor matts and the smell of wool fabric from the upholstery. Just running my hand across the seats brought back memories from my childhood. The cold metal dashboard would really crack your noggin if you weren't careful.

The driver asked me again where I was headed and I said that I really wasn't sure. He asked what I had in the old suitcase. I told him not much. He pulled off onto the side of the road, which had no apron and no painted lines separating traffic. "Show me what you got there in that suitcase," he said. I zipped open the old leather carry on and flipped back the top. It was completely empty. The good fellow said, "You can't travel like that. You'll never get anywhere."

He stretched out his left arm revealing his wristwatch. He proceeded to unbuckle its leather strap and said, "It's a Bulova, eighteen jewels," as he tossed it into the open leather suitcase. Next he retrieved a shiny silver name bracelet from his pocket and dangled it up for me to see. "You know what this is?" He asked. My name reflected from its silvery surface. I wore it for a long time. It was a birthday gift from a girl when I was a freshman in high school. I liked her a lot but her mom couldn't stand me.

"She was crazy about you," he said. I never knew that and I never knew what happened to that bracelet.

He tossed it into the suitcase along with the Bulova wristwatch. Next he pulled out my high school letterman's jacket with its large and small letters still attached and asked me if I knew about the jacket. I acknowledged that I remember the jacket. It still had the blue ink stain on the left leather sleeve. It was old but still serviceable. As he folded it in half and passed it back to the waiting suitcase I caught a whiff of my old girlfriend's perfume still clinging to it. Memories are like that.

This process continued with different personal items that brought back memories of forgotten times. With each item he would ask if I knew what the item was or if I remembered and each time I did. The last thing he produced was a wooden pencil. It wasn't a cheap yellow one but the more expensive kind with an off-white background and thin pinstripes of green and brown. He held it out in front of me so I could clearly see it. Then he broke it in half and tossed it into the suitcase along with all the other things from my past.

I knew what all the items were that were now in the old suitcase except for that new wooden pencil. So, I asked him who he was and why he broke that pencil and what was the point of breaking it. He said, "I am Irwin. I am your guardian angle. I didn't break that pencil, you did and you are the only one who can put it back together again. Life is like that, you know!"

The Last Stop

This morning when I caught the night bus, I noticed that the right front tire on the passenger's side was low on air. I asked Brad, the driver, if he would take me to where 'all the money was' and I mentioned to him in passing, that the right front tire was low on air. He nodded as we drove away slowly. We continued along a lonely dirt road for a ways before we stopped. Brad got down out of the bus and went into an old fashion gas station that looked like it was straight out of the 'Twenties', with its single pump out in front which had the large glass open sided portion that you had to pump by hand to fill to whatever mark on the glass you wanted to with the motor fuel they had on hand. There were no choices and no different grades of fuel. The sign said 'Five cents a gallon and no jugs please!'

Brad came out of the station followed by a skinny red fox wearing overalls and a red bandanna worn around his neck. He looked at the tire for a moment, then, he went back into the station and returned with a large brown bear. The bear only wore a greasy cotton cap tilted back on his head. He proceeded to lift up the front end of the bus while Brad and the red fox changed the front tire. Brad returned to the bus after paying the service station fox for the new tire, which looked more used to me than new and we proceeded on down the dirt road.

A while later, Brad stopped the bus and cried out in a loud raccoon voice, "Last stop." I was the only one on the bus and I was sitting in the seat right behind him. He must have thought I was deaf or maybe it was 'quittin time'. I climbed down the steps and the bus drove off slowly down the one lane dirt road instead of just disappearing like it usually does. There was a narrow footpath leading away from the road. It looked familiar somehow, so I followed it. The path led to a small summer home with a large covered front porch. There were three steps up to the wooden porch, with no handrail. I climbed the steps onto the porch. There was a single glider style chair by the front door. The door was open but the rickety screen door was closed. Inside there was a front room with an old cast iron potbelly stove standing out away from the corner on the right side. The room was small but cozy with its unfinished rough sawn plank flooring and cushioned chairs on either side of the wood-burning potbelly stove.

This front room opened into a small kitchen. The sink and counter were on the left side as well as a small two-burner stove and a tiny refrigerator. Two shaded kerosene lamps hung from the ceiling. In the corner was a small round wooden table for two, with its unmatched wooden chairs. At the far end of the kitchen was the back door, which led out to an old outhouse with its green paint flaking off and its door gaping open. On the right side of the kitchen were two doorways. The first led into a study with books lining the shelves on the walls and a small desk in front of the only window. On the upper left hand side of the desk were several books standing upright between two bookends. On the binding end of the books was the author's name, "Mayo". The second doorway opened into a small bedroom, with a single window and a plain single bed.

I went back out to the front porch and sat down in my glider chair. The old golden retriever climbed up the steps and lay down next to me and drifted off to sleep.

I was ninety-nine years old now, and this was my Last Stop.

Spindle & Glide

For two weeks the Source has pushed a single objective that involved for me first to 'square the circle', which I have done and second to create a spindle between the 'Druid' that is the source of all my seventeen incarnations and ' squaring the circle' that is composed of four corners and four characters in four different places at four different times: The Oracle in the cave of the Oracle; The Prophet in the cave of prophecy; The Connector in the cave of connections and the Buddha in the cave of the Buddha.

The bottom half of the spindle originates with the 'Druid' and the top half of the spindle connects to Captain England, a Star Ship captain from the future. Perhaps that will be my last incarnation.

This process of moving from one incarnation to another incarnation along the lines of probability and possibility is called 'Gliding' by the Source because it involves, so to speak, sliding 'down hill' without expending energy, from a place of higher energy to a place of lower energy. Ergo 'Gliding' is my next challenge with regards to re-connecting all of these seventeen different characters.

Key Stone

Not Key Stone Cop but the Key Stone necessary to complete my arch of seventeen prior incarnations across time.

Last night was the full moon accompanied by a full lunar eclipse. Every full moon, the International Order of Magical Crows hold a meeting, somewhere. Some times I go but it is always tricky for me, because I was once a member. I was once 'King' of magical Crows but they threw me out of the organization when I became a Wizard and was no longer just a sorcerer. They are two different things, very different things. Crows have black eyes and so do sorcerers. Wizards have glowing red eyes. That's a dead give away. Magician's eyes are sapphire blue.

I still maintain contact with one Magical Crow, a sorceress. Sometimes we meet at these full moon gatherings but I have to be very careful to keep my eyes closed so I don't stick out from a sea of black feathers. She couldn't see me but I could see her even through my closed eyelids, something a magic crow could never do. I made my way over to where she was with my blue eyes closed tightly and whisked her awareness far away into the mysterious magical forest.

She asked where we were. I told her we were deep in a magical forest. I followed her along a straight path of stepping-stones until we came to a clearing with a series of twenty-five stones arranged in a circle all about three feet apart. I know there were twenty-five because I counted them as I stepped on each one of them as I walked completely around the entire circle in a counter clockwise direction. When I arrived back at the starting point. I looked down at the stone I was standing on. There was the image of a knight in armor holding a sword and shield. I looked up and the sorceress was standing in the middle of the circle wearing a flowing, long sleeve, floor-length gown with a tight neck and no collar. She was holding a full sized bejeweled fighting sword in both hands. She raised it up and said, "This is the Ruby Sword. It is your sword" and she gave it to me.

She then turned into a beautiful horse the color of coffee with lots of cream. The horse hand no saddle. I was suddenly wearing a suit of armor. As I mounted the beautiful horse there was a sturdy saddle on its back with decorated stirrups. I rode down a narrow road lined with tall birch trees. I stopped in front of a castle on my left side, dismounted and moved up to the steps. I was welcomed warmly, by the beautiful queen with the bright-red hair. I bowed and presented my ruby incrusted sword to her. I kneeled and then was knighted by the queen as she said, "I Knight thee 'Sir Michael, Knight of the realm with the ruby red sword.

Go forth to serve and protect the citizens of the realm". I made the connection between the stepping-stone emblazoned with the emblem of a knight in armor and my incarnation as a knight as being the Key Stone, completing the arch of my seventeen incarnations. I was the Knight on the horse in the street in front of my house those many years ago.

Sands of Time

Last night, I went to 'The Place' to replenish my energy supplies. The Source was there. He asked me to walk with him. We were walking on sand. He asked me to tell him what I saw. I told him that we were walking on what looked like light, tan-colored sand that was completely flat. There were no dunes. There was no vegetation. The sky was absolutely clear. He said, "'The Place' where you get your energy from is actually 'a place' but a place that can be located anywhere. You have connected 'The Place' with what appears to be sand but it is in fact 'The Sands of Time", all time, the past, the present and the future. You did this on your own. Where ever you travel, 'The Place' will always be there for you". I asked the Source how this process actually worked.

The Source said that where we now were there was no time. Time existed on the other side, below the sand. If I wanted to go anywhere in time, I first need to go to the location of that specific time frame in the sand above and then tunnel down through the sand into that time and place to become a part of it. He left me standing there thinking about what he had told me. I gave it some thought and decided to go into the future to where my next incarnation will be as Captain England the commander of an advanced-space ship.

I specified a time before he actually would become the captain of a space ship, a time when he was still a cadet. I moved forward to that place in the sand and stopped above where I then began to tunnel down into the sands below. For me, it was reminiscent of when I was young and would chase what we called dust devils, catch them and jump into their middle as they whirled around and around getting ever stronger and stronger. Only this time I was boring down through 'the sands of time' into the future. This whirling tunnel surrounded me as I dropped down out of the sky onto the deck of a fast moving ship in the bay. I was in the midst of a waterspout. It dropped me onto the deck as it whorled away, back up into the clouds from whence it came.

They rushed to my aid and asked me my name. I was confused. John I said… John Scott. They shouted, "He's been hit by a waterspout. He must have a concussion. He doesn't know his own name."

"John, Scott, Fitzgerald…England," I stammered. I was now in the future, my future.

When I returned to 'The Place' the Source was waiting for me. He said, "You see… it works. Your Corgi, Lucy, was dying. You touched her and gave her the 'gift of life'. You see… the gift of life also works. Give of it freely to any and all who ask with no regard to the person or their life's situation."

Sepulcher

Last night, the Source and I were walking up a steep hill in a place obviously from somewhere in the distant past. He turned to me and asked if I noticed how easy it was for me to walk up this steep incline. I hadn't given it any thought but it was indeed quite easy when I should have otherwise been completely winded. The structures were made of stone, mostly limestone. Some of them were coated with white stucco or plaster. They were ancient but did not appear to be old. They were all in fantastic condition. When we arrived at the top of the hill, everything seemed so familiar to me.

There was a short white stonewall that ended against a sepulcher that had a simple stone cross sticking up out of its round dome-shaped top. Down below, I could see the town or city surrounding the hill. When I mentioned to the Source that everything seemed so familiar to me, he said that it should be familiar because I had spent much of my lifetime here in a prior incarnation. I remembered spending so much time hiding inside that stone sepulcher. It was my secret hideaway where no one could find me. Next to where I was standing was the entranceway into a stone structure. When we entered I immediately recognized it as my home, the place where I grew up.

A young boy about twelve or thirteen years old came over to me, picked me up and held me in front of a mirror-like surface. I was maybe seven or eight years old. He was my older brother. A tall woman with coal-black curly hair held up in ringlets wearing a white floor-link dress approached us. I immediately recognized her as my mother. She was always very stern and demanding with great expectations for me. There was another young girl present. She was a teenager but a few years older than my brother. I think she was my mother's sister. The Source reminded me that I grew up here in this house before I became the Emperor of Rome...Constantine.

Destiny

Last night the Source asked me to go with him. He said he wanted to show me something. I asked the Source if I should continue working on the twelfth attention. He said that I could now go there easily on my own but to be able to use the twelfth attention to modify health and well being outcomes was complicated and more involved than I thought. It would require more in depth work. I then asked about continuing my work on the use of 'Magic'. He said that I had successfully connected the sixth-string into the 'Cave of Connections' and subsequently established a connection from there to the 'Magic Mountain' but conjuring and the actual use of magic required a lot more skill and knowledge than

I had acquired at this moment. We stopped at a large rectangular space, smooth, dark and empty. He said he wanted to show me my 'Destiny'.

The Source suggested I think of this space like it was a holodeck, a place where things could be assembled seemingly out of nothingness. He began adding one layer after another and explained them to me as he proceeded. In the center of the space he inscribed a large circle. He began attaching different size lines to it. They were different colors and of different widths. He attached seventeen different flat ribbon-like lines to the circle. He said they represented my current life and sixteen others from my past lives. He then said that inside this circle was my death and all of the things that would happen during the remainder of my lifetime but this was not my 'Destiny' because I had a future incarnation as Captain England, a star ship Captain. Then he drew a single large, dark-purple line out from the perimeter of the circle off into the future. That life he said was my future. That was my destiny. I should disregard what awaited me in the rest of this life for that was not the destiny that awaited me.

Stairway to Heaven

Last night the Source asked me to walk with him. The odd thing about it was we were walking on a smooth transparent surface in the air several feet above the ground. As we continued walking along we were moving rapidly upward at a steep angle yet the surface we were walking on remained level. The Source asked me to tell him what I saw. At that point we were about a thousand feet up in the air. The landscape was dry and sparsely vegetated. The buildings were ancient but in mint condition. We were obviously somewhere deep in the past. He asked me if I knew where we were. I of course had no idea.

The Source said that I had been here many times before. Granted everything seemed familiar but I still didn't know where we were. He said, "This is the stairway to heaven." That didn't sound too good to me. He said, "You came here often in the past when you were the prophet Micah in a prior incarnation."

We passed through clouds and emerged in a grove of ancient olive trees. There was a small stream winding its way through the grove of old trees that was fed by a spring emerging out from beneath a bolder. The Source said the water was pure and holy. I asked where it went. He said that it fed the river Jordan. I didn't see how that could be the case.

The Source said that the stream became clouds. The clouds then created rain. The rain flowed into the river Jordan. I asked if this holy water was like the holy water in a church.

The Source said, "This is the only source of 'holy water'. It is pure. It is clean. You can drink it." I asked the Source what this holy water could do. He said it could do all sorts of things. I sprinkled some on my head and on my shoulder, which has been painful of late. You never know about things like 'holy water', so I took some with me to try it out and see what it might be able to do. I sprinkled holy water on a lot of people to see what it would do.

The Source said that this is where I came for these prophecies. My job had been to convey his messages to the Children of Israel. I was merely his messenger in a prior incarnation as Micah the prophet, from the years 740 BC to 670 BC.

Holy Water

When I went to Never Land, the next night, I was shocked to see that all the residents there whom I had sprinkled holy water on were now pure spirit. They had lost their 'Human Form'. That is a big deal. The challenge for me then became how to get them to the Re-assignment Angel without loosing them on the way or having something bad happen to them en-route. Some of these residents have been here many, many years. Now that they no longer had human forms they had to get in touch with the Assignment Angel and begin their next lives.

It finally donned on me that perhaps I could convince the Assignment Angel to come here instead of me trying to take all of them to her. When I asked her about that possibility she was more than happy to make a 'house call' and send them all on their ways.

There were only seven remaining residents in 'Never

Land'. They were Elizabeth Taylor, Michael Jackson, Selena, Fire & Ice and their two sons. They have all departed for new lives somewhere else in time and place. Now there are none. I wish them all 'God's speed' and the best of luck.

I asked the Source what is my next assignment was. He said, "Go to California and gather up all of those who have died in the California wild fires and bring them back to Never Land to recover. I did.

Sharon

Last night the Source asked me if I was ready to go on an adventure. I said yes. He told me to be sure to take everything with me that I would need for the adventure. I had no idea where we were going or what kind of adventure it would be so I went with an open mind. We came to this place that was very dark. He asked me where I thought we were. It was what looked to me like the cauldron of an active volcano with fire and brimstone and bubbling lava surrounded by darkness. He said it was the entranceway into Hell. He told me to save Sharon and left me there.

I have been to hell before. It is a terrible place but I went in looking for Sharon. The devils I encountered knew I was there so I traveled as pure awareness so they couldn't see me. I found Sharon. He was tied to a tall wooden post with his hands strapped behind his back against the pole. There was fire all around him and a personal minder-devil torturing him. I left but returned later to try and get him out of there. I brought a thick leather collar attached to a strong leash and holy water. I doused Sharon with the holy water and his body disappeared leaving only his tethered spirit for me to drag his spirit out of Hell with. When I materialized the minder devil came after me. I threw holy water on him and he exploded, disintegrating into a thousand pieces. After we made it out of there I took Sharon to the assignment angel. She was surprised to see me but very happy I had brought Sharon. He received the scroll for his new life and departed immediately.

I asked the Source what had happened to the devil when I threw holy water on it and it disintegrated. The Source said that the holy water destroyed the devil completely. It was gone forever. He was pleased that I managed to get Sharon out of Hell and survived the experience as well. I asked how Sharon ended up in Hell. The Source said that the period between when a person dies and when they get to their desired destination is fraught with all kinds of risks. Ariel had made a lot of powerful enemies during his lifetime. Devils were sent to spirit him away. I had successfully rescued Sharon.

Ariel Sharon, was born February 26, 1928, Died January 11, 2014. He was a commander in the Israeli Army from its creation in 1948 and became a General.

Itsacano Again

Last night the /source said, "Come with me." We usually walk but this time we were flying like Bat Man & Robin, zooming along through blackness and chaos. When we finally stopped he asked me to tell him what I saw. It was very dark and hard to see anything. He reminded me that had the ability to see in complete darkness so I could use that skill to see what was there.

I saw the face and hair of a dark complexioned Mayan man. The Source asked me who it was. I said it looks like Itsicano. The Source said that is correct, it is Itsicano a past incarnation of myself. Standing next to him was a short dark Mayan woman with a gold ring through her nose. The Source said she was my wife. Next to her was a boy about five years old. He said that was my son. Behind him stood a young girl about eleven years old. He said that she was my daughter. Off to the left side from her was an older girl. She was taller than me with light skin color. I estimated her age to be fourteen or fifteen years old. The Source said, "She is your slave. Free her and return her to her family. I will protect you. No harm will come to you."

I made the necessary arrangements for my family to stay with my wife's sister while I was away. The slave girl and I left immediately. We ran for three days and three nights before reaching her family. We were covering fifty or sixty miles a day. I returned the slave girl to her family then returned home as quickly as I could.

I asked the Source what the point of that whole escapade actually was. I thought it might be the 'Butterfly effect' or something like that. The Source said, "She had come of age and it was the right thing to do." The Source said I had already done it long ago in the past but he wanted me to re-experience the whole event again to help re-connect me with my incarnation as Itsacano, one of my seventeen past life experiences.

Quadrivium

In Latin this means the place where four roads meet.

Late in the morning around five a.m., I asked the Source If there were anything he wanted to show me. I was immediately surrounded by a fog bank. Out of the fog emerged a large tan-colored stallion with a tall man riding in the saddle. He dismounted and approached me. He was young, in his early twenties, wearing a dress uniform. The uniform was in good taste but not one that I recognized. He wasn't wearing a hat. His hair was dark and neatly combed. It was perhaps a bit on the full side for the military. The young man was polite and invited me to accompany him on his journey. We came to the top of a hill overlooking a village or small town. The structures were mostly one and two stories high, all plastered in beige earthen-colored materials. The streets were very narrow and paved in cobblestone. The village appeared to be middle-eastern from somewhere in the distant past. As we made our way along the deserted streets visible vapors of some kind were being released from the young man that drifted off in every direction. Eventually we stopped at a two-story structure with a round dome-shaped roof. I thought perhaps it was a small mosque.

The military man dismounted and bowed very low to me then ushered me through the entranceway. I passed through a narrow hall that opened onto a modest receiving room with a single large chair directly facing outwards towards the hallway. The chair was reminiscent of a large throne but it was plain and not at all elaborate. Sitting in the chair was a large fat man wearing a gray, hooded robe. His face was hidden within the hood. In his right hand he held a fat wood staff. His bare calves and grotesque feet were visible. To me he was reminiscent of the grim reaper. In an instant I was back in my own bed. The Source asked me what I had seen. So I told him. Then he asked if I knew the meaning of what I had seen. I said that it was an allegory and explained what I thought it meant.

The young military man represented youth, beauty and strength. The magnificent horse represented the ability to travel anywhere with ease. The vapors effervescing from the young officer represented the corona virus as it snaked secretly through the air throughout entire villages. The fat humanlike hooded creature represented death from corona virus spread by the young officer throughout the countryside and citizenry. The Source was pleased that I understood what the allegorical message was. Unknowingly youth were spreading this deadly Corona virus everywhere.

For several days the Source has encouraged me to simultaneously stay in the cave of the Oracle, cave of prophecy and cave of connections. When he asked for my comments about those requests I told him that I thought I should also be going to the cave of the Buddha high up on the side of the mountain. He was very pleased and said, "You have squared the circle. You have closed the Quadrivium. On your own you have connected the four caves. Now you and they are as such, one."

The ultimate point of this book "Saving Seventeen" was for me to reconnect with all seventeen of my past incarnations.

The only way to save oneself is by saving others.

Books by: Dr. Mayo

The trilogy of 'Coincidental Journey', 'Untold Story', and 'Wizardling', is about Lucid Dreaming, Dream-walking, Shape-shifting, Sorcery, Wizardry, Magic, Time Travel and the Power of Illusion.

'Coincidental Journey'   Copyright 2015
    ISBN # 978-1-940985-16-9
    Completed in 2015; awaiting publication.
'Untold Story'   Copyright 2016
    ISBN # 978-1-940985-42-8
    Completed in 2016; awaiting publication.
'Wizardling'   Copyright 2017
    ISBN # 978-1-940985-73-2
    ISBN # 978-1-7345741-3-5   e-book
    Published and released in: April 2019
'Robin'   Copyright 2018
    ISBN # 978-1-940985-55-8
    ISBN # 978-1-7345741-5-9   ebook
    A 268 page book of Elizabethan poetry.
    Published and released in: April 2018
'Oracle'   Copyright 2018
    ISBN # 978-1-940985-95-4
    ISBN # 978-1-7345741-6-6   ebook
    Published and released in: December 2018
' Vision Quest'   Copyright 2019
    ISBN # 978-1-7345741-0-4
    ISBN # 978-1-7345741-1-1   e-book
    Completed in 2019. Published February 2020
'Art of Magic'   Copyright 2020
    ISBN # 978-1-7345741-2-8
    ISBN # 978-1-7345741-4-2   e-book
    Completed in April 2020. Published July of 2020

'Saving Seventeen'   Copyright 2020
   ISBN # 978-1-7345741-7-3
   ISBN # 978-1-7345741-8-0 ebook
   This book is about saving the living and the dead.
'Star Quest: Navigator'   Copyright 2020
   ISBN # 978-1-940985-74-9
   This book evaluates several exoplanets located
   within the habitable zones of their star system
   for intelligent life and Human habitability.
   Completion date slated for 2020.
This book evaluates several earth-like exo-planets located within their star's life zone.
Completed in 2020 & is awaiting Publication.

About Dr. Mayo

Dr. Mayo was born in Tucson, Arizona where he maintains a private dental practice located in the heart of Tucson, which is limited to the treatment of children and special needs patients.

Dr. Mayo practices: Dentistry; Hypnosis; Astral Projection; Dream-Walking; Shape-Shifting; Sorcery; Wizardry; Illusion & Time-Travel.

He is currently exploring the "Art of Magic" and the "Twenty-six strings" that make up String Theory
(**Current**
Incarnation) Dr. Michael Thomas Mayo

(**Future** Incarnation will be as a Starship Captain:)
Captain John Scott Fitzgerald England

Seventeen Incarnations

Oracle   2000 BC
Micah   (prophet)   740 BC to 670 BC
Druid priest   (I Druid) 3rd century BC
Egyptian Priest 2nd century BC
Claudius (Roman Emperor)   10 BC - AD 54
Roman Soldier   AD 200's
Constantine (Roman Emperor)   AD 306-337
Buddha   (from the mountain side cave)
Sebatini   (The Traveler's Buddha)
Itsacano   (Son of 'Heart of Gold')
Sir Michael (Knight in armor)   AD 1115
Ignasius of Loyola   AD 1491 to 1556
Shakespeare   AD 1564 to 1616
Joseph Silverstein   (1600's)
Ship's Surgeon   (1700's)
Venice Merchant   1800's)
Wild West Cowboy & local Judge   (1850's)

Notes

Notes

Notes

www.ingramcontent.com/pod-product-compliance
Lightning Source LLC
Chambersburg PA
CBHW071221080526
44587CB00013BA/1452